THE FLOWERING GUM

A mother's path from grief to peace . . .

Alexandra Browne-Hill

BALBOA.
PRESS
A DIVISION OF HAY HOUSE

Cover design by: Liam Aidan Browne

Balboa Press books may be ordered through booksellers or by contacting:

Balboa Press
A Division of Hay House
1663 Liberty Drive
Bloomington, IN 47403
www.balboapress.com
1 (877) 407-4847

Because of the dynamic nature of the Internet, any web addresses or
links contained in this book may have changed since publication and
may no longer be valid. The views expressed in this work are solely those
of the author and do not necessarily reflect the views of the publisher,
and the publisher hereby disclaims any responsibility for them.

The author of this book does not dispense medical advice or prescribe the use
of any technique as a form of treatment for physical, emotional, or medical
problems without the advice of a physician, either directly or indirectly. The
intent of the author is only to offer information of a general nature to help
you in your quest for emotional and spiritual well-being. In the event you use
any of the information in this book for yourself, which is your constitutional
right, the author and the publisher assume no responsibility for your actions.

Any people depicted in stock imagery provided by Thinkstock are models,
and such images are being used for illustrative purposes only.
Certain stock imagery © Thinkstock.

Printed in the United States of America.

ISBN: 978-1-4525-1398-0 (sc)
ISBN: 978-1-4525-1397-3 (e)

Balboa Press rev. date: 10/13/2014

THE FLOWERING GUM
A mother's path from grief to peace . . .

This is a handbook for all people that have experienced the death of a child. It is an emotional and inspirational recollection of grief of a loved one, and accepting that they will always be with you in spirit. That is insight and acceptance. This is the Gift.

Ms Rene Barics
Registered Medium, Reiki Master/teacher, Medical Intuitive, Spiritual Healer and Counsellor.

Death is nothing at all.
I have only slipped away into the next room.
Whatever we were to each other, that we are still.
Call me by my old familiar name.
Speak to me in the easy way which you always used.
Laugh as we always laughed at the little jokes we enjoyed together.
Play, smile, think of me, pray for me.
Let my name be the household word it always was.
Let it be spoken without effort.
Life means all it ever meant.
It is the same as ever it was;
There is absolutely unbroken continuity.
Why should I be out of your mind because I am out of your sight?
I am but waiting for you, for an interval, somewhere very near,
just around the corner . . .
All is well. Nothing is past. Nothing is lost.
One brief moment and all will be as it was before only better,
infinitely happier and forever.
We will all be one together.

CARMELITE MONASTERY

INTRODUCTION

Although I thought I understood death to some degree, through both years of nursing and personal losses, when I lost my son mere weeks before he joined the rank of "man" . . . I stepped into a hazardous journey of emotional depth and incredible learning.
It was not long until I discovered that I had understood nothing at all.

From the first moments of shock and hope, to the desperate wish to turn back time, along with the trappings of desire to deny the truth, I travelled this treacherous path. I was not alone. The world wept with my family and me for the many losses and heartaches surrounding us all on a daily basis.

The world may have wept but it fully intended that I had much to learn. What possible things can we learn from grief? One way to discover the answer to this question is to write the road travelled and gain the gift of logged hindsight. Although I had no such plan to do so, eventually a book appeared.

Reading this book is very confronting and some have told me apologetically and with hesitation that it is too difficult to continue reading. It was never my intention to share such rawness at the time of "The Greatest Trauma of My Life" however, life plays funny little games with people in order to share a message. When eventually I began to follow the signs, I could not only see the importance of the "Greatest Trauma of my Life" itself but the direction of helping others that this Event led to!

Each Event had an Event attached to it what's more, culminating in the longest, most exhausting six years of my 52 years and yet . . . this is where I have gained immeasurable wisdom, peace of understanding and the benefits of feeling a loving connection with a Supportive Universe, yes, against all odds.

Please be brave and keep reading to the end. The Flowering Gum is not a long book but it highlights the choices we all must make one day if you have not already had to. We can choose to get lost in our agony or we can choose to understand it. There is no easy road but there is direction we might all benefit from if we want to walk it and *The Flowering Gum* is simply one way to move forward.

Although I have tried many times to rewrite "The Flowering Gum, a mother's path from grief to peace", or even embellish it, it must stay the same as my original diary. My beloved son Kieran has decreed it so.

And therefore it is.

EPILOGUE

Years ago, I would lie on my side in my bed and quietly watch the tree outside the bedroom window. It stood rather precariously on the curb, a little too close to the edge of the road.

It had grown into a mature and well-shaped tree despite its obvious hardships. The limbs were a bit windswept and gnarled, the tree squat and perhaps starved of water. When it flowered however, this Flowering Gum defiantly blossomed with beautiful and prolific red, spiky flowers.

I thought it a magnificent tree. It seemed to me that this tree had survived a lack of water, nutrients, even a comfortable garden site and needless to say, love yet this flowering gum bravely continued on giving shelter to the biggest of God's creatures and a home to the smaller ones. People, dogs, cats and mice scurried towards this tree for comfort. Birds hopped onto its branches, chased each other with screeches and snuggled into the branches in cold winds or sweltering heat.

For several years, with broken heart I would lie and absorb strength and calm from sharing a quiet time with this tree. It never let me down. My divorce was painful and becoming a single mum with tiny new baby Bridget and two gorgeous boys, Liam at six and Kieran at three was not part of my happy dream. I grieved for a long time. This tree became my lifeline.

One day I came home and found that the local council had cut it down. I cried and grieved again.

More recently, I have another special tree to watch. Our Kieran left us to reside with God and now visits us instead. On his 18th Birthday, we had a tree planted for him. This gift was dependent on the Board of the Cemetery and only allowed because that very month, a tree had fallen in the entrance of honour. We were told that we may plant a tree in remembrance of our son but although we were to pay for it, the Board would choose the tree. We accepted these terms without hesitation.

On the occasion of Kieran's birthday, we hurried to see the tree that was planted on our behalf. The plaque was to be added later.

We were greeted by the beautiful sight of a six foot sapling alongside the honour road. It was to my delight, a Flowering Gum. There are other Flowering Gums running alongside the dirt entrance road and I often look up high to inspect these wonderful trees. They are healthy and happy. I note how settled they are into their protective roles as homes, shelter and strength to the needy. They provide joy and calm to the residents of the cemetery and soothing to those that ache.

When people ask me about Kieran's tree, I tell them this . . ."If I can't watch the boy grow up then I shall watch the tree grow instead." Each visit to Kieran entails a little trip to check on his Flowering Gum.

I watch it blossom and grow strong with tall limbs. I am still calmed and given strength by this little sapling's determination to grow huge and unwavering just like its peers. The flowers remind me that life can be beautiful and despite the odds, it is worthwhile finding the courage to keep going.

One day, Kieran's Flowering Gum will be huge and I will remember our young man both as the three-year-old lad and as the 17-year-old teenager. The trees that have guided me through my life have never let me down.

This journey of Kieran's and mine pays homage to our connection with nature and homage to God, whoever He is perceived to be, for giving us nature to soften the blows.

With love, Alexandra

A Moment in Time

We stood in front of a small, beautiful, natural waterfall in the bush and exchanged our vows. Our special event was attended quietly and without fuss by a tiny group of family and friends—and the dog, who kept running off to sniff the wildlife. Your dad Martin and I began our married life with little in the way of fanfare or expectation. Everything seemed so simple then.

With excitement, we were blessed two years later with your brother, our beautiful, blond firstborn son, Liam. Then one cold winter's day, we added to our family with you, our lovely second-born son. I encouraged your arrival into the world by jumping up and down in road puddles while it poured rain. Our gumboots filled with water, and Liam happily chortled despite being incredibly soggy. We felt very lucky. We were very lucky.

It is funny how life turns out. You just do not know what is around the corner. The simple plan you started with becomes complicated, then messy, and eventually you are on a different plan altogether!

Your dad and I lost the plot somehow when you were two and we parted.

In my distress, I failed to notice that I was pregnant. I badgered my doctor for blood-test confirmations within days of conception with both you boys, I knew I was to be your mother before I was supposed to! They were annoyed, but I was right! I missed my intuition cues with Bridget and didn't expect to be a single mother giving birth to my third child on my own.

Nonetheless, your cute little sister arrived by caesarean, and then there were three. I later remarried and added two stepchildren into the mix.

So here I am years later, thinking about our life, Kieran—and your death.

I suppose I could write, "Once upon a time, there was a very ordinary mother and her son . . ." or even just write myself some angry and often defeated notes on the senselessness of losing someone I love. Instead, I find myself writing a journal to you, Kieran. There is so much I want to say to you and teach you, not to mention share with you, but it is all a bit difficult, because I don't exactly know where you are. It seems that I am always losing you in some form or other.

For seventeen years, you have had me turning in circles, making sure you were all right. Do you remember that you climbed out of my car window as a little boy and disappeared into the crowds? Or the four hours that you were lost on Australia Day at a festival filled with thousands of people? Your dad and I found you with the help of the police and the emergency services. You were sitting on somebody's shoulders, eating ice cream and smiling your magic smile at us as if you had never left our sides. You were completely unfazed. Unfazed? Well, I was fazed! I put a wrist lead on you after that, but still your passion for exploring led you away from us.

Only this time, Kieran, it led to your death. So then, if I cannot share hot chocolate, cuddles, and chitchat with you, I shall write to you. This journal is for you, Kieran.

Today is 6 May 2007, a month after that traumatic phone call. On Good Friday, not long after midnight, you—my baby, only seventeen years old—lay trapped beneath Daniel's four-wheel-drive Toyota Land Cruiser. To readers who might choose to share this journey of tragedy and personal growth, I report that my Kieran, also my friend and soother, my second-born son, passed on four days later in Melbourne's Alfred Hospital.

Thirty-one days ago, a 7:30 a.m. phone call from my ex-husband, Martin, turned our lives inside out. Our stomachs still churn high in our chests, and food will not slide down our throats easily. My head feels like mush, my body aches, vision is blurred, and limbs heavy. I ache for my son, whose life has been dramatically shortened and years stolen from us, his family, and loved ones.

This is our story, Kieran's and mine, and the journey in grief and discovery that we together have shared. A caring friend gave me a journal in the week we lost Kieran, but it was to be another few weeks before I found time to continue my writing to Kieran in it. Meanwhile, Kieran's birthday arrived mere weeks after the accident, and being his eighteenth, therefore an important birthday, we went to extra effort to celebrate it.

Thus, we begin with this bittersweet event.

13 June 2007

Happy eighteenth birthday, Kieran! 13 June 2007—4:14 p.m. You were born at 4:10 p.m. exactly eighteen years ago today. You were a beautiful baby. You looked just like your father. You arrived exactly on the expected date, as though by prior organisation.

You were an irritated baby, though, and the nurses took you away to give me a rest; then they brought you back to give themselves a rest! It turned out much later that you needed chiropractic treatment to straighten the bones in your neck following our difficult birth. You did get stuck at the shoulders, after all, and had to be "yoinked" out! Although your mood improved, you still proved to be relentlessly impatient and often demanding, which was a trait you maintained for the rest of your life.

Today we held your eighteenth birthday party. You know that, of course, you were there. Your dad, your stepmom Fran, stepdad Mal, brothers Liam (also known as Bill) and Chris, sister Bridget, best friends and neighbours Debra and Nat, Karen and Kingi Horua from next door and my hometown in New Zealand, close friends Liz and Pauline, and I met at the cemetery at 11:00 a.m. It was raining, and I prayed for a little sun.

Your friends had obviously been down to visit you already. There was a can of Bundy and Coke, and cards with flowers. Had you still been here, your party would have been a noisy and busy one.
We gathered in coats beneath umbrellas and read your new plaque. Your dad had spent ages deliberating over the words and found the perfect tribute for you.

It read:

Kieran Shae Browne
(13.06.1989—9.4.2007)

There's rum in a battered old billy,
The pannikins placed in a row . . .
Let's drink to the next merry meeting
In the place where the good'uns will go . . .
Now and then in the shades of the twilight,
When the soft winds are whispering low,
And the darkening shadows are falling,
You must think of the young lad below . . .
All wrapped up with stockwhip and blanket,
In his land 'neath the Southern Cross glow . . .
Our Kieran sorely missed & deeply loved.
Not gone from us, just gone before us . . .

We all placed beautiful flowers on your grave.

There were two photos and a Deniliquin tag 2006 left there from your mates, Daniel and Tash, in memory of your trips away on Ute musters, and a windmill from your step-aunt Elder. We hugged, laughed, and took photos. We all took a wander up the hill, past the variety of trees, to the older part of the cemetery, where the gazebo is.

Together we provided morning tea between us—coffee and Fran's homemade biscuits. Hope you like your birthday gift of a six-foot sapling, a flowering gum planted beside a huge rock. A plaque will soon be added to the base of your tree that refers to your eighteenth birthday. We all wrote messages on helium-filled balloons and sent them off to you. Happy birthday, Kieran! You are eighteen now!

We took more photos and went off to Shanikas in Berwick, an Italian restaurant. It was a beautiful meal. They provided a lovely ice-cream cake full of chocolate and a special birthday plaque on it in chocolate. Some of us sang, and some of us cried. More precisely, I tried to sing "Happy Birthday" but choked and cried, which pretty much choked up the house. Sorry, guys! On we went with more photos and coffee. We enjoyed a lovely day, Kieran, lovely, despite the obvious.

I spoke to your best mate, Mick, last Friday. I like him, Kieran, very much. He was on the train to Bendigo when I phoned him. All your mates were meeting in Bendigo for your birthday reunion, and tonight they are meeting at the pub for your birthday tea. I think it is great!

Tara, your ex-girlfriend, phoned last night and told me that their family is visiting you at the cemetery tonight too. Mick also mentioned he is visiting you after work.

You are so loved, precious son of ours. You have left a trail of love and impact everywhere. MySpace on the computer is buzzing with Kieran and lovely letters still. I am very proud of you; you have a wonderful heart and give so much. Thank you for choosing me as your mother. I miss you terribly, though, it is a horrible thing to look out for a loved one for years, and suddenly they are not there. It hurts, but I continue to trust that you know you are loved, and I still hope that you will share in family events. I know you attended your birthday today. I can feel you around.

Your Uncle David, I know, greeted you on the other side. I cannot thank him enough for the gift of support. Tell him I love him. So my son, again Happy 18th. Your dad shared whisky with you today! Enjoy your party with the boys tonight!
Love always, Mum

18th June, 2007
Yesterday was two months since we buried you Kieran. I cried all day. All I do is conjure up your beautiful face in my mind and tears appear. I miss you. Easter is entirely different now – none of us can eat the Easter Eggs and I finally threw them away with the hot cross buns.

I am going to try bit by bit to reconstruct your story Kieran. This is dependent on how I go with this . . . my heart aches.

Thursday, 5th April you were home some and out some. You had recently secured an appointment with a horse trainer to take you on as an apprentice farrier on the other side of Melbourne in Flemington. You were going the following Thursday on the train.

You also had an eye appointment in the city to try and be pronounced colour safe for acceptance into the army. Being colour blind has always given you certain disadvantages and being unable to serve in the military may have been one of them, although you were not certain whether you wanted to join up or be a man of the land. "I don't know that I want to be shot at, mum" you offered me in your latest opinion of your future. "I'm sure you don't" I responded with great wisdom and no small amount of relief!

When I arrived home from work, you came to ask if I would drop you at the hotel for tea with the boys. I dropped you off in Berwick with your friends.

At 11pm, you popped back in to pick up your swag (you and I chose it at Rays Tent City and you paid for it with your first pay. This was in readiness for your trip to the Ute Muster in Deniliquin.

You wandered into the house with your suede boots on and I was in bed. You ducked your head around the door and asked (but really told) me that Daniel and his girlfriend Tash were outside waiting and you were all going camping in your usual camping spot. I berated you for wearing your boots on the carpet and you gave me a wry grin with a tiny shrug of your shoulders, typically Kieran! Eerily enough Mal stood behind you and was frowning with great reservations but I only hesitated a moment. This is a regular camp site I thought, and it is a long weekend. Daniel is older . . . they should be ok.

Boy was I wrong . . .

Off you went, up to the hills of Tonimbuk.

I did not wake until early Good Friday 7.30am when the phone rang.

Your father was telling me that you were in a coma in the Alfred Hospital. I could not grasp what he was telling me and the fog would not lift. "Can you tell me that again please, Mart?" I asked several times. He patiently repeated himself while the damn message sunk in, "Kieran was flown in at 2am-ish and still can't breathe on his own." The police had woken Martin and called him into the hospital in the middle of the night.

Why didn't they call me right away?? Why wait until morning?

It seemed that Tash had been driving up to the gravel road, where she stopped and you jumped in the tray. Daniel drove on. We don't believe that there was any alcohol or speeding involved but somehow, on a bend the Ute tipped . . . a heavy 4 wheel drive Toyota Long wheeled base rolled on and pinned you my beautiful son . . . *Shit, Shit, Shit.*

I gather that Daniel and Tash were shocked but uninjured and tried to free you. There was panic, darkness, and phone problems, and the rescue crew were given the wrong road name. The panic and stress must have been phenomenal. They tell me that you were conscious for the first hour while Tash tried to keep you awake and gradually you faded into a coma.

Finally, finally an hour and a half after the accident you were flown by helicopter to the trauma department of the Alfred Hospital.

There is an investigation – Tash and Daniel told their stories and the Crash Investigators will be on the job. We were told that things would come out in court months and months later.

The phone call shocked me Kieran . . . . I knew right then that this was it!

This was *the* moment you have always told me about. **No!** My Son . . . my little boy, I'm not ready . . . not yet, please God, not yet! I couldn't speak and the tears choked me. I knew. You told me at six years old that you would not be here long. You told me several times over that your lifetime would be short – that it was . . ."Mum, I'm not going to be here long. I just know." "Mum, I don't want you to cry for me when I've gone . . ." I believed you. For years, I feared for you. I wish I had been brave enough to hear what you wanted to tell me. I should have been able to discuss this with you and you gave me several opportunities. I wish I had.

I called your grandparents to warn them, knowing deep down that we would lose you.

I phoned your big brother Liam and without hesitation, he rushed home. Liam had already approached me several weeks back, out of concern for you Kieran. We felt you were living your life a bit on the adventurous side and Liam kept an instinctive worry about your future tucked away in his heart.

I called next door too, of course. They came running. I phoned Mal who was on a bike ride in the city and I cried. He rushed immediately to be at your side.

I couldn't move. I couldn't stop crying. Strange for me, huh?

It was to be two hours before I could get my body into a car and head for the city. I just could not function. The knowing weighed me down like lead. Liam, Bridget, Natalie, Karen and Kingi waited for me silently. Nobody told me to hurry. They all just waited. It was weird.

Then when I could get going, Kingi drove Liam and me, with Karen to the hospital. With my hand in Liam's, and looking out of the car window at nothing, I ventured to ask God if I might keep my son . . . please, please . . . and I received an answer!

A terrible and soul tearing answer.

A loud and irrefutable "*No!*" reverberated above my left ear. It was not in my head, nor did anyone else seem to hear it. However, it was without a doubt, a very firm and definitive *No*. I chose to take the path right then at that moment, of hope but God help me, *I knew*.

I am actually writing this account of your last days in the car. I am parked in the cemetery and looking over at your grave site. It is raining and I have already been in my coat and boots and placed more bright flowers down. I tidied up and stopped for chats for 45 minutes. I love it here with the quiet and beautiful trees filled with nature's birds. I find a tiny bit of peace for a moment to ease the deep sense of fracture within my heart and soul.

So there I was begging God to let me keep you and He gave me warning.
My heart sank.

Arrival at the trauma centre:
You weren't there! Martin, Mal and you were still in the Emergency Room. They still hadn't stabilised you enough to transfer you. By 10am, Good Friday, they had you on the respirator and you still couldn't breathe yourself or respond to any stimuli. You had been to theatre and had exploratory surgery – they found and repaired a hole in your bowel.

You already had developed black bruising from the bottom of your back to your thighs with a massive swelling of the right buttock.

We waited.
At 11am, you were finally transferred to the trauma unit and again we waited while you were settled in.

To see and touch you was an event of some relief. Your dad and I took a hand either side of you and began our preparations for supporting you.

The first obstacle to overcome was accepting you lying there with nine IV lines and two blood lines being poured in, and a machine breathing for you.

Watching your chest rise and fall unnaturally with loud noise and the dialysis machine whirring away emptying the toxins was something we soon had to come to terms with.

You were bleeding due to reduced clotting and no-one could work out why. Many, many tests were done over the next few days. You bled from your eyes, mouth and nose – quite worrying. However, we caressed you and talked to you, trying to find the best place to stand and still be near you. Not easy with all the staff and so much machinery. The staff were unforgettable. I see each of them in my mind. They tried so hard for you.

Dr Meagan was gentle and caring. She called us together for a meeting. She carefully described each of your injuries and what that meant for your prognosis. She prepared us for the possibility of a sad outcome by telling us "Kieran is as sick as a person can be and still be here." However if you pulled through the next 24 hours, maybe there would be hope.Well what a rollercoaster ride.

Of concern was your coma – not drug induced, so were you brain damaged? You solved that for us soon after . . . !

Nick, Liam's best friend and his mum Katarina visited the hospital with backpacking friends Dania and Anna-Christina and we all took turns to visit you. Nick came running through ICU and grabbed my hand . . ."Quick, Kieran just moved his arm and opened his eyes."

I ran all the way along to room 13 and there you were fighting the tubes down your throat. Clever boy. Liam and I took turns to speak and reassure you. When Liam told you to "relax man", you stopped struggling. You went back to sleep.

I had found a spot at the back of your head where I could wrap an arm around your chest and place my face into your hair. I spoke into your right ear until I remembered that was your bad ear. You had ruptured an eardrum with a nasty ear infection a few years back and had residual loss of hearing in high tones. As I reached over your head to speak into your left ear, Liam yelped, "Mum, he's opening his eyes!"

This was the moment we let you know that we were there with you. It was also then that we fully established that you weren't brain damaged, because you did follow a few simple commands. Unfortunately, you slipped back into your coma and that was the last time your beautiful eyes opened for us.

That afternoon, still Good Friday, Daniel and Natasha visited. They had just left the Pakenham Police and the local hospital. Daniel came in with tears running down his cheeks. Both of them looked pale and washed out. Much of the day was spent in the waiting room taking turns to visit you. I took Daniel by the hand and into the room where he stood looking at you and trying to tell you to get better. He spent some 10 minutes trying to find the words.

Later, it became necessary for me to inform him that I didn't hold any negative feelings against him, but both fathers were exceedingly angry with him for whatever shenanigans had occurred that resulted in your accident. Both fathers wanted Daniel and Tash to leave. They did leave but I felt sad about that. Obviously, they had suffered a terrible time too. However, I could not deny that

Daniel shouldn't have allowed you to be in the tray – what were you doing in there?

And so the waiting game continued. Late in the evening, Katarina and Liam got a lift home with Nick. Daniel and Tash had long since gone. We three parents began to settle in.

At another meeting with Dr Meagan, we were prepared for further surgery – the bleeding still wouldn't stop and a further exploratory operation of the gut and a debridement of the clot, which was now huge on your buttock, would be next.

Monday, 9th July, 2007
Three months ago today since you left us. I managed to get through a normal day without too much drama, largely because I spent ages with you yesterday. Mind you, you are always on my horizon and in my thoughts 24/7.

Last week was hugely difficult because things have been slow to sort out. I still have bills to follow up with TAC, your birthday tree plaque to look out for, chasing the arrival of your birthday rose bush from back in June and phoning the Coroner's office because your death certificate still is not available. The Coroner's office is unable to tell me why you are having special autopsy tests done and what they are for. I phoned Denise, the Senior Constable to find out what this all means and she too is a bit uncertain. However, miraculously the Coroner's office phoned me to say that finally, finally, your results would be back in a week. Then the death certificate and related paperwork will be generated in over a fortnight. This has been unsettling and tear provoking.

Some days are pure Kieran days and although I do not mind them, they are painful to get through these periods. Sure enough, another Kieran event occurred with the arrival of a letter from Daniel, inviting us to his and Natasha's engagement – what to do? I don't blame Daniel for your death Kieran, but other's do. What if I go to this party and find I'm wrong? I'm uncertain how to respond. I need to think it over some more.

Yesterday was very, very wet and cold but I was desperate for Kieran time. A cuddle would have been great. I donned boots, gloves and a coat and set out to tidy up the grave site and feel your presence. I knew you were with me and it gave me strength. Thank you.

11th July, 2007
Another tough day – your Aunty Mandy, my sister, visited yesterday and we went to Fountain Gate Shopping Centre. Some-thing simple like visiting the National Geographic shop and looking at Aussie/ camping goodies was quite difficult. I had wanted to go down to the cemetery, but it wasn't nice to take your visitors down there! So even with the sun shining, I didn't visit my boy.

Next came the phone call that stated that your first ever tax papers were ready to put in at tax time, which must annoy you no end! That little shock came before the next little shock . . . . The letter box held an envelope from Pop containing photos of your beautiful, shiny, wooden casket being lowered into the ground by your dad, Mal, Liam, Chris, Uncle Harry my brother; your cousin Josh, Matt and Tamaiti Horua. That one hurt.

Some days are just more painful than others. My chest still hurts, sleep doesn't come without heavy sedation and my stomach still feels like it has rocks in it. Every so often throughout each day, a memory of you Kieran, arises unbidden and my gut clenches. More often than not, it is accompanied by a very rude and angry expletive . . . if I could somehow turn this all around and do it all again differently – maybe I could keep you with me longer. Even though your death may not be my fault, it is a mother's curse that I feel I have failed to keep you safe. You were born to me and placed in my care . . . how in God's name did this bloody mess happen?

July 2007. Back to the Alfred

These memoirs are taking so long to put into place – I have to be so careful about when I start. I'm now working full time again and running around after Chris and Bid, so finding a quiet time when I know I won't be interrupted is very difficult. I feel that I need crying space as I write so this must be allowed for.

It gets dark at 5.30pm these days so going down to the cemetery after work is no longer an option and I certainly don't think it's a good idea to write to you before I sleep – breathing after crying at midnight doesn't make for quality sleeping!

So, we got up to Good Friday evening when you were not improving and you were bleeding everywhere. Blood was pumped in constantly and the doctors were anxious. We were told to go on home and rest, and if you worsened, we would be called in. We did come home and check on everyone. It was quite late and the kids were surrounded with friends. Matt, Nat, Liam, Bid, Chris, Nick, Dania, Anna-Christina, all in various beds and on mattresses snuggled together giving comfort to each other and generally finding their own meals. Karen and Kingi of course called on us and fed us, checked on us and shared our painful vigil every step of the way. They had phoned their son Tamaiti and he worriedly phoned in every few hours for updates.

Easter Saturday

On arrival early Easter Saturday, we were met by the doctor whom told us we were to prepare for the worst. Would we like a priest? Yes, we would. Together all our family, with the Horuas next door, prepared our last rites with an open minded Catholic Priest. We spent a few minutes with readings, prayers and a song. Suddenly before we finished, with the kids huddled together, the doctors interrupted. Please wait outside again. Result? Another operation – check the bowel again. Inspect the rest of the internals. Where was the bleeding coming from? Your clotting factors were not working.

When you were returned to us, you now had your abdomen left open with a wound vac in place. Your bowel was swollen but no signs of further damage. However, all your electrolytes were out of sequence. You had "crush injuries" – every doctor's nightmare. Patients with crush injuries suffer a change in metabolism – the tissues begin to die and slowly the body builds up toxins. Eventually the organs begin to fail because they cannot continue to filter out the huge amount of poison. This was so, in your case. Whilst you were in O.T., the enormous swelling of your right buttock had to be released. Beneath the skin, a massive clot was removed and beneath this, sure enough was crushed and damaged butt muscle. This wound too, was left open and covered up with tegaderm.

The difficulty here was that you had already built up so many other toxins from being under that Ute for so long, that you were now too unstable to keep in the operating theatre for any longer. Removing your butt muscle would have to wait and risk rising toxins. You were re-scheduled for Monday. You seemed to rally a bit on Saturday despite . . . or maybe because of your last rites. By the way, at your last rites, Kingi held your feet and prayed in Maori. We had Liam, Bridget, Chris, Natalie, Karen, Kingi, Martin, Malcolm and I with the Catholic Priest. It was really lovely and peaceful and somehow gave me, at least, great comfort.

Your father held much more hope than I. I've since heard that you didn't tell him you would die early. You will have had your reasons or, of course, maybe he didn't want to hear you. Whichever, he struggled and wanted none of the negative thoughts. Rightly so!

I might say here that as I sat with you, holding your hand and rubbing your heart that I had a moment of great anguish on Good Friday night. I cried and begged you not to leave me.

Only weeks before when we were discussing your future, you took me in your arms and rocked me, wiping away my tears. You told me, "I will never leave you mum. I will always be here for you." Even at the time, I wondered in what form those words were to take. I had felt deeply disturbed about your future and could not place a reason because it is always wonderful planning things with your children. I'm seeing a clearer picture now! Bridget claims you told her that you would be leaving this earth at 17 – why didn't you tell me? I would have believed you. I would have given up work for you even. Time was of the essence and I was so unaware . . . so unfocused . . .

I think that I believed you might die early as you kept telling me but I felt it might be several years off yet . . . not 35 years before me! Jeez Kieran!

. . . Back to the Alfred . . .
By the time we left the hospital very late on Easter Saturday night, we began to hope. I started to think about your rehabilitation. Without a butt muscle, you would be handicapped. However, you have beaten the odds before boy, so why not now? I imagined giving up work and spending the next year driving in and out of the Alfred. We would take turns, your dad, Mal and I and help you through the exercises of learning to walk again. We planned our plans and dreamed our dreams.

Meantime, both nights now I had taken your old bike riding shirt with Fox on it to bed and wrapped myself in it. Not that we slept.

We felt so sick and worried, and in a daze. Then came the early morning call that one dreads. Come in folks – Kieran has taken a turn for the worse. Hurry! So we hurried. We picked up a parking fine, which later on, a kind social worker reversed for us. On arrival, your father had beaten us there, looking fatigued. Again you rallied with us there to cheer you on. We hoped and prayed for an Easter Sunday miracle.

Incidentally, before we left the house we left an Easter egg on each person's pillow and brought yours in for you. Did you know that during all this time, Mal was being the rock? He watched our backs, Martin and I. Brought us coffee, made us eat, ran interference, made regular phone calls to the outside and generally did what was required. He put his own heart on the back burner. I have always told you he would do anything for you.

What came out of the contact with the "outside world" were hugely different culture prayer groups. It was quite lovely and interesting. Even in the throes of heartache, I took note that we had Rumanian Orthodox candles burning for you along with Germans far away on the other side of the world saying prayers, Maori prayers, and Catholic Italian candles – messages from far and wide. Amazing!

I found a beautiful photo of you from last year at School and placed it in a frame given by the Horuas. Matthew found Kingi on his knees blessing your photo in tears. This photo was later buried with you. Your Maori 'dragon' that you asked me for in Rotorua and we gave you for Christmas 2006, I gave to Kingi, whom spoke to the Maori Elders and this tiki was blessed. We tied it to your wrist on Friday and you wore it the entire time. The blessings and prayers were *abundant*.

And so, Martin, Mal and I stayed with you all of Easter Sunday. From time to time, we took little walks to the hospital park across the road for coffee breaks and cigarettes. Mal did not complain when I "borrowed" one of Martins' smokes! Liam, Nick, Katarina, Dania and Anna-Christina visited at will.

Your blood pressure began to drop. Meagan, your doctor was struggling by now to find ways to bring you back to a good chance of survival. She spoke to us every few hours and carefully updated us with the latest. I worried incessantly that you were in pain and unable to express this. Dr Meagan promised me that you were not. I tried to feel reassured on this issue at least. Everyone involved in your care lovingly tried to warn us how precious your situation was. And yet no-one would give up either. Megan approached the Professor of Trauma and they began to treat you with unorthodox procedures. All weekend, the blood products poured into your body. At this stage, you now had two dialysis machines and *every* trauma monitor and machine that could be used. Every appropriate drug had been administered. You continued to have lowered clotting factors and high toxins. Your blood pressure was dropping and your pulse pumping away madly trying to fight back.

The nurse in me was busy registering all these facts. The spiritual side of me had already been told by a Higher Soul what would happen. The human strength bit of me was busy staying calm, washing you, loving you, singing to you and holding you. This bit felt accepting, patiently waiting, enjoying the moment and busy storing things away for future journal writing. The mother in me however was screaming deep down, down in my core, with disbelief and a profound indescribable pain. The core of central agony that drags one to their knees is then sheathed by a thick blanket of raw and bleeding ache, which is then wrapped in a layer of sadness then another layer of anger, then denial mixed with disbelief. So layer upon layer, it rises from where it settles at the solar plexus, growing in layers until your gut clenches at one end and your throat burns at the other. The mother department went into automatic pilot. I could not touch the truth. I was going to lose my baby, my second born son, at any time.

Meagan ordered the administration of Methylene Blue (X-Ray dye) into your drip in order to raise your blood pressure. We needed you to rally enough to push out the built up toxins. And guess what? It worked! Again, we dared to hope. Martin went home that night and left you in our care. He was exhausted and in turmoil. He needed sleep and we knew he wasn't likely to get much. However, we hoped you would rally nonetheless. Steve, your night nurse, on his arrival to night shift however, warned us that you couldn't keep going like you were. Despite the fact Kieran, that you always battled hard for that extra mile, extra foot, extra inch . . . I knew Steve was right.

Mal and I took a break down in Prahran for some sort of meal, which I couldn't eat and instead began to cry over. The poor man in the Turkish shop couldn't begin to imagine what was wrong. "Lovers tiff?" I wanted to tell him "My son is dying and my heart is dying with him . . ." but of course, I told him nothing and in fact didn't much care what he thought so deeply distressed was I. Mal sat opposite me saying little, his eyes full of pain as he tried to will me on.

So we returned to your side hoping for another night with you, then another day perhaps . . . and then another. We settled in after all the obligatory phone calls to the kids, next door and parents – updates all round. (The Horuas were feeding us all at whim up to this point and plates of food kept appearing in the fridge.) We began a series of reading stories to you – your dad had begun a book about a jackaroo and his adventures, so he, Mal and I took turns to read it to you. The nurses put a radio in the room for background music, some of it western music. I settled myself in my usual spot with a stool placed at your head, my left arm resting gently around your neck and chest and my face resting against the right side of your head. Being scrunched up in this position caused backache but I couldn't get enough of you to cuddle. We told stories, read, sang songs with Mal at your right side, stroking your arm. We listened to your breathing, the sounds of the respirator, heavy and laboured. The monitors beeping and clicking on the dialysis machine echoed around the room. The BP machine alarmed each time your blood pressure raised or lowered too far and the many IV machines alarmed each time a flask of fluid, bloods or medication ran through. The nurses did not falter. They moved confidently, efficiently, attending to each task. The hours moved on. Mal left the room for coffees regularly.

The first couple of days we were asked to leave the room for any required activity, but the nurses had long since stopped asking. We now came in and out of room 13 as we needed.

Up until now, I had remained strong, focussed and practical. I sent prayers and love, and talked to you all the while. But I knew time was running out. Salty tears ran down my cheeks and into your hair. It is my belief that you knew I was there and you too, felt the deep and growing grief. Several times, I wiped away tears that rolled down the side of your adored face, into your ears.

So the night wore on – a mixture of impending knowing and dread, with hope that you would continue on and find a way back to us. These next bits of my memory are very difficult to write and cause me great anguish. As I begin to creep forward with my thoughts, a pain sharp and hot develops beneath my left breast. My heart clenches with the trauma and I know that this will take me days to tell.

29th August 2007

As you can see, I am jumping backwards and forwards around the diary. Today is a full moon, as was last night, which makes it five lunar months since you left us for the other side. I remember the redness of the moon clearly and recall that it seemed so fitting to end such a day. Today, or more precisely last night was a lunar eclipse. (People seemed a little wacky today so that explains it!) Five months without you Kieran (in the ways we wish anyhow!) and the pain hasn't lessened and I haven't learnt how to cope better or 'get over it', or any other human logics. I simply bury it all deeply to be pulled up and examined closely and nurtured, but only when there is time to patch up the emotional mess that follows. Sometimes I get to choose the examination time, and sometimes I don't. Either way, I guess I am not going to feel any better until I spit out this section of our story Kieran . . .

Our last night together rolled on with me alternating between reading to you and crying into your hair. I made your hair salty and sticky uppy . . .

As I always did, I informed you that I would go and have a little coffee break and return shortly. Imagine my shock this time when you responded by wildly shaking your head! Up until then, you hadn't moved . . . so, okay my son, I will not leave you. Our time together became more precious and more urgent by the minute. Therefore, Mal and I stayed where we were.

Then later into the early hours, as nausea crept in and my need to straighten my back heightened, I became a little desperate. To leave you for a minute was a minute lost. Mal looked terribly ill and I felt horrible. I had developed headache and backache from holding you whilst sitting on a stool at your head, leaning forward over equipment and lying forward to keep my cheek on your hair – one arm thrown across your shoulder and around your chest. I could not physically get any closer for all the machinery in the way. I needed to stand. I needed a drink. I needed my heart to stop shattering. My God, how could this whole scene be? This is just a nightmare of the worst kind.

I had levels of emotional existence that were very clear to me:
Nurse mode came first – coping, ensuring your needs were met, washing your face, drips continuing . . .
Care mode – talking to you, having you know that I was there. I would not leave you.
Physical mode for us – knowing we had a long journey and the need for fluids and food.

Shock mode – shelter from facts.

Beneath . . . deep abiding grief.

As time slipped by, physical needs struggled to the fore. Mal had developed chest pain and I became torn between two precious family members. Mal refused to go and rest. When a couple of hours later, I told you that we were going for a wee walk, you shot me another message! This time, your nose gushed a fountain of blood before I completed my sentence. Okay, okay Kieran. I told you, I am not going anywhere. I began to clean your nose and face. Oh my baby, we both knew what was coming didn't we?

We stayed with you. Mal popped out and collected coffee. We waited with you more. I read to you, cuddled you, sent thoughts to you, and loved you. Previously yesterday or maybe it was Saturday, I felt that your spirit had floated above your body, but today, I felt that you were in your body and waiting with me until it was time.

Finally, Mal and I needed to go for a break. Mal looked sick. We decided an hour would help. I told you we would be back and you didn't respond. I hoped and prayed that you understood. Mal and I wandered down the hall and found our way into the visitor's waiting room. We found some blankets that Steve, your night nurse put out for us. We swallowed a coffee, toileted and made a nest of blankets. Exhausted and aching, I fell into a light slumber, still feeling the hard floor beneath my aching back. Mal had settled into the slow breathing of the deeply weary. Suddenly, with a bang, your face appeared in front of me. You were calling me. I knew you wanted me with you. Time was passing. My heart was heavy but my body was heavier at that minute. To force my arms and legs to get up was a major feat. I sent a mental message to you. "I'm coming!" Mal woke and asked me if I was okay. I merely told him, "Kieran wants me" and made my way back to your side, slowly and sluggishly. Sorry about that Kieran – bodies can be such a nuisance.

Again, I cuddled into you feeling now that our souls were beginning our goodbyes in earnest. We waited. Past 6am, Mal was suffering chest pain. I needed to make a choice. I spoke to Steve. Amazingly, he felt that "Kieran has hung on and his BP is up – maybe, maybe he has a chance." Suddenly, it seemed that I had time. Time to duck home and shower; have a small sleep then return. When Mal entered with another coffee, we talked about heading home for a while. Time was being kind – time, my enemy.

By 6.30am however, my soul had other ideas. As if there were two people in my body, I leaned forward holding you tight. "Kieran, you are so tired. If you need to go, it is okay. I love you, but it is time to go. Wait for your dad, then it's okay to go." With that, feeling calm and right, I told you I loved you and collected my belongings. Person number two however, felt great that we could have a sleep and shower then return for today's battle. I called across to Steve and including you Kieran, cheekily told you both not to get into any mischief and left. Numbness set in.

I contacted Martin, by now 7.15am and he let me know that he would be with you in half an hour. Home again, children and friends were everywhere. Your brothers and sister had support everywhere, people sleeping in any spot of our house and dishes covered the benches. I had a shower, and then came out for a drink. An SMS arrived from Martin – 'Kieran has been seen by the Professor. They want to operate on him.' Operate? You weren't strong enough to operate on! This is weird. So I asked via a phone call to Martin. "Is he strong enough?" I queried and Martin answered that you must be. Another renewed blast of hope in this game of emotional ping pong.

Then at 9.20ish, the phone rang and the doctor at the Alfred was phoning me. He informed me that you needed surgery or you would die. He hesitated then said that it would be very uncertain whether you would survive the surgery so frail was your condition. I already knew this. "Go ahead" was my answer. Go ahead my darling second born son. Don't leave us. Numb. Numb.

Kingi appeared in the dining room where we were congregated. Mal, Liam, Chris, Bridget, Natalie, Dania, Anna-Christina then Karen. Later I discovered that Kingi had a feeling that he needed to be next door. Then the phone rang. Twenty minutes after the first. It was the doctor. "I'm sorry" he said "but Kieran hasn't made it." Kieran gone. (You waited for your dad as I asked you!) Well Kieran, we knew didn't we? You didn't want or need another operation sweetheart. You just needed to go Home. I knew that.
The doctor was apologetic and kind. You didn't even make it to the theatre. I felt the deep anguished wail that rose out of my core and into the Universe. The death of my beautiful son that meshed tightly with the death of a part of my centre, a part of my soul. A necrotic piece of my soul that will never repair.
Kieran, I understand . . . and yet I don't understand.

The next phone call was from Martin . . . shattered and alone . . . "I am on my way now" I told him. Two car loads – all of us back to the Alfred to say goodbye. Numb, quiet, shocked and aching.
Today is 9th September 2007. Five months on.

You died on Easter Monday. A new star appeared in the sky on Easter week Kieran. I wouldn't be surprised if you had something to do with it!

Back at the Alfred

We arrived at the hospital – quiet and subdued, just hurrying into room 13. Liam went straight into Martin's arms. I went straight to you. The room was quiet without all the machines beeping and buzzing. The only noise was that of the suction, trying hard to drain out all of the excess fluid that built up in your body. There was so much of it because your organs failed to filter. You fought so hard for us Kieran and gave us the opportunity to accept and say goodbye. Like me, Liam and Bridget knew you had to go – you told us many times. However, Martin and Mal (and everyone else) did not have the benefit (or liability) of knowing where this Easter was leading. I had spoken to the senior nurse about an NFR order the evening before you left us. This means an order "Not for Resuscitation" should you flat line. The nurse asked me straight out if I wanted to do this. I thought a moment and replied that everyone had worked so hard to try and save you, that it wouldn't be fair to take away that last chance. So, no to the NFR. Malcolm sighed with relief beside me and later told me that he thought your should decide your own outcome. Too true.

And so with your fate decided and your body still and cool on the bed in front of us on Easter Monday morning, the sun streamed through the window of a magnificent blue skied day.

The sound of sobs and sniffles with the gentle suction were the only sounds. I was dimly aware that Mal, Liam, Bridget, Chris and Martin were comforting each other. I had eyes only for you. I began to memorise in earnest – I kissed your lovely face and played with your hair. My fingers traced your facial features, storing away each detail. I ran my hands down your arms, chest, hands and legs.

I checked your knees. How many dressings did I attend to on these knees? I know your knees so well Kieran! Amazingly, your left knee damaged with grazes by Ute Scooting had finally healed while you were in hospital (which we growled at you for incidentally, since skating in your boots in the dirt while holding onto a moving Ute is hardly a safe idea now is it?) Great I thought, we got your leg better and now you can't use it!

With my memory inspection all zipped up, my super efficient person stepped up with great gusto and began to respond to the staff. Firstly, the doctor came in and I helped fill in the death certificate. He told me there would be an autopsy because they weren't really sure why you didn't respond to their great efforts. He told me that your case was a TAC case with the Coroner's office and police involved, and that all these parties would be contacting us. "Okay" was all I said.

Two beautiful nurses came in to check on us. I asked one for scissors and a plastic bag which she supplied, the only bag she could find being huge! I began to cut your hair and place it in a bag. Gross you say? Mums are weird Kieran . . . but you did tell me you wanted a haircut remember! . . . Next, I asked for a stamp pad and the nurses came back with folk paint after great fishing around! They wanted to do this for me. Together, the three of us painted your feet and hands and made foot and hand prints in green and red. These became my prized possessions. Your poor hands were so swollen. We had difficulty stretching out your fingers for a clear print. I was dimly aware that the family were gathered together, mostly around the window. Liam leaned on the window sill looking drawn and defeated. He and Martin murmured together from time to time.

I continued to chatter to you honey boy, as if you were there. Sometimes smiling politely to the staff, sometimes busy gathering your belongings and our things together . . .

A mother bustling around, as if nothing were wrong . . . I didn't feel much I guess, except at peace that you were now resting without pain and exhaustion. From time to time I felt the need to look up inexplicably almost expecting you to wave goodbye, but each time I was disappointed.

If I'd had the ability to see you, where would I have seen you, I wonder? Mentally, I sent you a sad "I love you" and hoped that you got it. Please God, please gather my boy close to you and keep him safe . . . We filed home silently – I do not even know what time. All of us were too tired and shocked to do any more than huddle together silently.

And so the rest of our lives, broken and tattered, began. There were no tears to cry – not yet. Four days ago, we knew our outcome. Years ago in fact, we knew our outcome. At least, that's what you mentioned at least five times Kieran. At some level, our spirits knew.

I began the process of phoning the people closest to us. The remaining children continued on huddling into the support of best friends, girlfriends and each other as needed.

I continued phoning but didn't linger. Facts, simply told with a reassurance that I would inform each of service details as I knew. Coroner's court cases and autopsies take ages, holding up one's carefully laid out plans.

I told both Mum in Queensland and Dad in New Zealand not to hurry over as yet because it could all take days. "Hold off until later" I said. This I knew would grieve them more because they couldn't be with us. An additional complication was the fact they had endured a divorce and having them both staying here at the same time was impossible. I put the problem aside for now.

Another source of worry was the fact that my boss (one of my dearest friends), had finally managed to get away for a week for the first time in two years. I had kept my small work unit informed via Anne my nurse friend, but made the decision to let my boss rest. I knew she would be angry with me, but she had worked so hard and her family deserved some undivided attention for a few more days. I stressed over when I should tell her, until finally a few days later I found that our friend and work Technician Gary had told her by phone. She was deeply upset of course and it goes without saying that I made the wrong call with this decision . . . although I could plead insanity I suppose! I am not known for my conventional thinking after all and I can almost see you rolling your eyes!

Martin kept your Uncle Harry informed and he had several times been into the Trauma Unit to check on us all. Did you know he had been in to see you Kieran, aching for you? You both had quite a soft spot for each other.

Auntie Mandy was teary and supportive. She told me that she had seen the nightly News segment of the accident on television depicting the site with your swag slung across the ground, the Ute upside down. She hadn't known then, that it was you, fighting for your life.

Kingi arrived from next door to inform us a meal was being served in your honour Kieran. We all filed over. Karen had put heaps of tables together under the pergola that you helped build, son. Food aplenty graced the table. Both our families, with all our family extensions gathered around, Mal and I at the head of the table. Kingi made a loving statement of our loss and Matt his son gave a lovely speech. It was a magnificent meal and a special way to see you off. We were surrounded by those we love and told stories of your misdemeanours Kieran . . . of which there were plenty! Liam and Nick meanwhile flipped food between themselves like twins!

Much wine and reminiscing later, we wandered back over the fence to our humble abode. In looking up to the sky to talk to you Kieran, I saw to my amazement the most stunning, blood red full moon. It was huge! The sky was alight and the moon announced an important event.

God has an Earth Angel return to Him. What a banner Kieran! I instantly knew that your passing was special but of course, don't understand how.

You fell into a coma at the beginning of Easter and passed on the last day of Easter with a full, red, huge moon and a new star is discovered . . . and you knew in advance! I wondered to myself whom you might actually be, then berated myself since I couldn't be that lucky and honoured as a mother. But of course, I am that lucky and honoured because you chose me and we were so close. Kieran, you are not only my second born son, but also my friend, my pride, my worry, my everything. I need you here for me to be complete.

The grief will be relentless and nothing can prepare me for the journey ahead. I took sleeping tablets and wrapped myself in your Fox mountain biking shirt which smells of your sweat . . . and tried to sleep.

Tuesday, 10th April, 2007. Looking back.
I was up at 7am and poured a coffee. Nobody else was up yet. I took a sip and the phone rang. That was the first and last fluid (or food) that entered my mouth until midnight. The phone ran hot and the doorbell rang incessantly. I didn't move from my seat at the kitchen table where I took the calls. News moves fast. I had kept a dozen people informed from the hospital unit yesterday via Anne, Karen, Kingi and Harry. People were checking on us. It felt like a dream, no sorry . . . a nightmare. I took call after call giving information with

no emotion. Everyone was very kind and I felt enormously grateful that so many cared.

Sometime during the day, I collected the phone diary and began to make my way through it. A problem became apparent. Kieran, you went to three different schools and I'm not certain anymore who are friends and whom are not! In the end, I phoned your friend Matt in E.H. and shocked his mum by asking permission for her son to chase up your mates for me. By this time, the computer "MySpace" was buzzing and news began to travel even faster. All you kids are close and share friends, so this awful news flew! My mobile took 187 calls and each of you kids chalked up to 400 calls by the end of the week.

Martin and I had agreed to keep this day as a rest day but it just wasn't to be.

I phoned Martin G. the Pastor of our local Church to inform him of our news and also left a message at the Church itself. Already I had decided that your service should be there. You had received your Achievement Award from school, attended archery and gone to youth group at this church. It seemed right. Martin G. phoned back immediately and offered to conduct your service when the time came. It was a perfect idea as he knew you. We arranged to meet at the church the next day. I phoned our Martin. The calls then continued until late into the night.

Wednesday, 11th April, 2007. Looking Back.
The household was quiet still but the phone calls continued. Flowers poured in. Your stepsister Aimee had gone to Portland last week before Easter to visit her mother for the first time in over a year and was supposed to return, but didn't. Nor did she phone us at any stage to discuss her plan of reuniting and then living back with her mother. We thought she was going for a brief visit then coming back

to resume her hairdressing apprenticeship. Instead she caught a lift back up here to spend 10 minutes with you in your coma, and then disappeared again. She returned with demanding rudeness for the day of your funeral after ensuring that we paid for her travel by train (twice since she missed the first train!) then left again in a flurry of self-importance, and to this day, I haven't seen her again. We have lost two of our children in a week. Can our hearts break any further?

Martin, Fran, Mal and I met with Martin G. and a church representative and discussed a service. We all seemed to agree and fit in with each other. All we required was a date. And a funeral director.
Pulling out superficial happy faces still wasn't too hard at this point, because being busy was happening without us! We were given the name of "Bethel Funeral Services" as a not-for-profit group of Christians whom provide good care at the service and send any profits to charity overseas. Again, marvellous.
Church – tick, Pastor – tick, funeral service – tick, afternoon tea – tick . . . ahh, cemetery.

I wrapped up in the beloved Fox shirt with some downed sleepers and turned in. Enough. It was to be another four months before I stopped clutching that Fox shirt.

Thursday, 12th April, 2007. Reflections.
Last night you paid me a wonderful visit! Dressed, freshly out of the shower, I began to leave the bathroom when a cool gust of sudden breeze messed up my hair and the smell of you went straight up my nose. There were no windows open, and anyway, I had my nose in your hair for days on end so I knew you instantly! I know you visited me! Thank you! I called out a "hello" to you as you swung past. In my ignorance however, I laughed, thinking there would be tons of

those types of visits! I didn't understand how much energy that visit must have cost you. *But I loved it*! I felt so happy to have contact.

The afternoon was booked with a representative from Bethel Funeral Services at our Martin's place. I was told by Martin, whom booked with Bethel, that I was to bring the things with me that we wanted to bury you in. The hunt was on . . . where are your suede boots? . . . Where's your chain with the Celtic cross? . . . your best jeans weren't clean (again, you grub!) To clean them or not . . . where oh where is that chain? I picked up your spectacles so you can read, your front door key in case you want to come home and nobody's there to unlock the door, and your belt with your favourite buckle. I did not care that anyone might think I was strange. I felt it was important that these items of everyday use remain with you. The extended family, God love them, did not say a word and later on I felt very grateful for their tolerance. Perhaps one day my behaviour will add to my very long list of what to tease mum about!

Our Bethel representative was wonderful. He was professional, but gentle. We chose a beautiful, simple, wood grain casket with gold handles. The wood was lovely. We decided to put your bulls horn sticker on the lid (you were saving it for your Ute) then asked our rep if we could park you in our local Cemetery. He phoned, and to the surprise of some of us (thinking our nearest Cemetery is an old pioneer cemetery and probably closed), it was arranged that we meet the Management from the Cemetery Trust and see what we thought.

Several difficult phone calls yesterday revealed to us that your autopsy was to take place over an unknown period of time. Without really knowing why, but feeling comfortable with it, I had arranged the funeral service for Tuesday, 17th April, 2007 (eight days after you passed over). Together with our ever helpful Rep, the four of us carefully arranged the details of your service:

Venue: Church of Christ
Date: Tuesday, 17th April, 2007
Time: 1pm
Afternoon tea: 2pm
Burial: Cemetery lawn section
Procession: 3pm

Finally, having completed all of the finer details that we could think of and having organised a time to meet the carer of the Cemetery, that left the hardest job of all. I was suddenly rendered weak and powerless when it arrived time for me to hand over your possessions. I began to cry, shaking, needed to reach out to Mal to help me empty your clothes into the arms of the Bethel representative. The thought of someone else dressing you for the last time was deeply, horrifically painful. You were to wear your newest boxers and socks, singlet (blue bonds of course), your new R.M. Williams shirt you just recently bought and your best jeans . . . yes, dirty. I handed over your belt with an R.M. Williams buckle . . . but couldn't find your beautiful tan suede R.M. Williams boots. (Much, much later, I found out they were cut off you and ruined.) Meantime, I gave your work boots – all dirty, as both fathers felt this was a good representation of your hard working personality.

And so with all that taken care of, we all headed down to our chosen cemetery. Oh my God Kieran! What a beautiful place to rest in. There is so much love in this cemetery. You can feel it. There are beautiful trees, a zillion native birds, views of the hills . . . perfect. I can visit you straight from work!

We chose a spot in the lawn section, but close to the trees, where you can see the hills of Upper Beaconsfield. Remember I took you and Chris up there with your bikes so you could both practice your jumps? It feels so right. The manager was wonderful and helped us with our arrangements, which included plans for a plaque. Done.

Friday, 13th April, 2007.

Things were starting to hot up. Mal and I dragged our sorry arses to the hairdressers for a tidy up. We briefly exchanged sad hugs with the girls in the hairdressers. They all knew you and had often cut your hair.

Graeme, Mandy, her boys and mum were all beginning to filter in. Karen and Kingi, as always made the trip to the airport to collect mum. Mandy was taking her down to Bairnsdale for a couple of days. Kieran, I had no idea what to do with the situation of my parents! They each wanted to know what they should arrange, but didn't really want to spend time together. I didn't have any savvy answers, so finally rang your Uncle Graeme and Aunty Mandy and asked them to take care of the problem. They immediately rallied around to help. The family were wonderful. They couldn't do enough.

Martin phoned to say that your autopsy had been completed and your body would be released to Bethel on Monday, ready for your funeral service on Tuesday which of course was booked.

I had already known how your service and burial would be – it seemed to be pre-planned somehow. Everything fell into place with a sense of rightness. It all felt so . . . so 'Kieran'.

I am reminded that I have dreamt of speaking at a funeral on several occasions over the years so there is nothing in this planning that seems strange . . . which is in itself quite strange. Yet there is no difficulty in this planning. I just know what must be done. It feels completely natural.

Flowers, cards and phone calls continued to flow in. People finding out and phoning shocked and horrified, people making arrangements, people checking on us . . .

Dad and Shirley were to arrive the next day. I decided not to stress about where people were going to sleep or what we were going to eat. All the social niceties in the world felt so unimportant. Despite the fact that all seemed pretty organised, the undisputed fact of the matter was we were all in a deep shock. It feels like standing in a phone booth trying to hear what is being said outside.

The days began to sift together a little bit. The end of the day always ends the same way . . . with the family eating little, looking pale and worn, each quietly retreating in their own way. For me, by after tea time, I am in the shower on my knees sobbing. The black hole in my being was bottomless and the anguish indescribable. My baby should not have to endure these terrible things. It is my job to protect the beautiful beings that I have created – my babies. I have failed. My heart is torn to shreds at the merest notion of your journey. I cry for hours each night, until Mal drugs me and pops me into bed.

And so we drifted on, in a daze towards your funeral service.

You again visited me Kieran, in a beautiful and welcome way. I sat one morning, upon the front seat of our patio, staring blankly at nothing and missing you. It was cold with winter coming and the light wind was chilly. What a lovely surprise to have a warm kiss tucked in a sudden warm breeze, arrive on my left cheek. I can still feel where your lips landed on my face. I love you too. You made me smile, yet again.

Over the weekend, the family filtered in. Mal and I had visited Martin and Fran to arrange the photos for the Powerpoint section of the service. We also tapped into the church again. Shopping for clothes was next for Bridget, Liam and Chris.

Aimee was making arrangements to return for your service but was not staying with us. At this point she was barely acknowledging us . . . after asking us to pay her way. Glad we are useful for something. I did at one point after her arrival on Funeral Day, ask her to delay her decision to move until we could catch our breath but she seemed to look right through me. I did not have the energy to investigate any further.

Funeral Day
Tuesday, 17th April, 2007
This was the most momentous and heart rendering occasion of my life. (The other momentous but joyous occasions were of course giving birth in the first place!) Our beautiful son, Kieran Shae Browne, 17 years old, was loved and honoured in a most beautiful and loving service, attended by hundreds and hundreds of people from everywhere. The church held 1,200 people and was nearly full. I had often wondered where you got to half the time and now I knew! So many people.

We as a family were truly honoured. People shut their businesses for the morning and attended. For me, the CEO of my current work, the CEO of my past work hospital, their staff and the staff of two doctors' clinics where I once worked, all shut shop and paid their respects to you. Most of them had seen you for dressings and post trauma x-rays after your various falls along the way! Kieran, bikes and trees were always an ominous mix!

The music was a mixture of "Kieran" – a Ute mustering welcome, with a welcoming song sung by Nat and Bridget, *Hope you had the time of your life* by Greenday. Bid threw back her head and laughed at the end which was beautiful to watch. I gave a little Kieran run down and some thanks. I had so much to say but wasn't able to think clearly, so I hope it was okay. Aunty Pauline held my hand. Martin G. gave an introduction talk, which was great. Our Powerpoint presentation showed 50 photos of Kieran to Fureys music "*May we all someday meet again.*" Crying could be heard around the room. Liam was in most of these photos with your arms around each other. He hurt so much.

Kingi gave a Maori reflection with memories of you as a hard and honest worker and a wonderful young man. How true! Your dad gave a sensational talk towards your friends about loss, learning and taking care. It was talked about for days.

Martin G. focused on a talk about Corinthians 2 1:16, "Love is patient and kind" – pointing out that Kieran was kind, but definitely not patient! It was an honest but love filled service that was just 'so Kieran.' It felt so right. I hope you liked it Kieran. Your bull's horns on your beautiful western looking, red wood casket looked fantastic. Your dad went yesterday to Bethel Funeral Directors to put it on. He also checked you were dressed right and said his goodbyes. We had your R.M. Williams Akubra, your photo, stockwhip and Aussie flag on your casket with some Eucalyptus. It looked great. These things were taken aside to be buried with you. To the Maori Farewell "*Now is the Hour*", your male family members escorted you to the hearse. Liam, Chris, Matt, Tamaiti, Harry, Josh your cousin, Mal and Martin.

The attendant stepped towards me and handed me your photo . . . a moment of time I shall never forget. Your face, your eyes stared up at me. I saw with deep clarity the loss of my own, born of my body . . . I crumpled. My family swung into action and caught me. Fran from the left, Mum from the right and Mandy from behind. They all threw their arms around me. The attendant prompted – no one can leave until you do . . . I rose and followed the boys. I began shaking. Fran on one side and Dad moved in on the other. I pulled myself together for the next bit.

What was the next bit? People. Hugs by the million . . . people for an hour and a half. So many loving and caring people.

Daniel's parents were beside themselves. On the way into the service, Daniel's mum fell into my arms sobbing. She kept saying, "I'm sorry, I'm sorry . . ." My heart broke for her. How horrible. Many, many tears. So much sadness. So much love.

Kieran, it was a splendid service and so right. We heard that your service was the nicest service that people had ever been to. I hope so because that is what you stood for: Love.

And so on to the burial.
Bethel placed your hat, your photo and Maori carving into the casket as per Maori way. (Your Easter egg and other things went in too.) We had kept the burial to family, due to youth numbers. We felt that hundreds of friends in our little cemetery would be a bit much, so maybe 40-50 of your family and dear friends followed the procession. Martin G., in conjunction with Bethel, arranged a special and loving burial. Your Grandma Beth read a special piece called *Do Not Weep*, and the boys lowered you down. This was without doubt the hardest bit. It signifies an irreversible truth and destroys any hopes of being caught in a horrible dream.

Therefore more tears were generated. People cuddled and ached. They began to filter away, to meet if desired at Kingi and Karen's later on for a wake.

Our family stayed back a little. I walked through the cemetery, reflecting on the 17 balloons we gave to the young people to let loose during the burial ceremony. They flew high and gave us a small sense of your new freedom. As I walked, I was swooped by a beautiful parrot that screeched. I smiled. Already, I was sensing you nearby.

The Wake

Kingi had discussed with me how important a farewell dinner is. It disturbed him that I hadn't wanted to do anything. Finally, after thinking it all through, I agreed to the notion. Karen and Kingi again stepped up and took the enormous task of providing a meal for family, extended family and friends. I had ordered Turkish takeaway via a friend at Narre Warren whom was visibly distressed at our awful news. He had only seen you a couple of weeks ago.

Pauline and Lisa did a great job of organising, pick up and arrangement of food and joining Karen in providing a venue, drinks and hospitality. We have such fabulous friends. Malcolm gave a welcome speech and the night began to flow. Your dad and Fran appeared I'm pleased to write because originally they were going home to a quiet house. As it turned out, we had a little fun to see you off Kieran.

With all my family together, with our parents, our siblings, our nephews and niece and all our friends, work mates and neighbours, we gathered and drank to you. I don't know if there was a speech. I'm sure there was. I was beyond noticing. Later, much later, we crashed into bed. There was nothing else to do. There were no more ceremonies to hold . . . and I couldn't change God's mind and bring you back.

Aimee spent a small amount of time at your wake Kieran, and then arranged a lift with her Uncle. She is on the run again. Back to Portland without any support towards the family or wanting any from us. She declined to come home and wanted to move her belongings out on this night, of all nights. I refused to let her take her belongings away on the day of your funeral. We kissed her and let her go.

Several days later and I woke feeling beautiful. I dreamt that you were before me. Except it was so real. Your face was looking down at me. I reached up and felt your face, ran my hands over your chin. "I love you" I said. You were peaceful and it emanated through me, surrounding me. I knew you loved me too. As Mal delivered coffee to me, I stretched and told him "Kieran just visited me." It felt so peaceful and warm.

Two and a half weeks after you moved in with God, I made an appointment with a Medium who draws people's Spirit Guides. I knew of her from our visit to the New Age Expo earlier this year Kieran. You and I went along to see what was there and I was intrigued by the idea of someone seeing my Spirit Guide.

Especially since I often felt that "someone" is watching over me. A few years ago, I went to a Psychic for the first time. She told me that a male Guardian Angel sat at my left. He had long brown hair, was bearded and wore a long dark robe. I was to call him 'Teacher.' I remember being a little disconcerted because during all my years of feeling watched over, I had always assumed it was by a female. Maybe my lovely best friend Alice whom died when you were little, or a grandparent? My life went on and this information drifted into my past.

On the day of my appointment with the above Artist Medium, I was desperate to talk to you. I was consumed with ghostly images of you waking up in your casket and panicking. I dreamt of you being 'lost' in space. My imagination set off and I could not settle. I was so unhinged by thoughts of your terror that I actually forgot that you had gone through an autopsy, which pretty well confirms one's death I would think!

Nervously, I drove to the other side of town. The Medium told me that "the carpet had been pulled out from under me." She began to draw. On a big piece of cardboard, a face appeared with the use of crayon. A man with long red/brown hair and a reddish long beard looked back at me. He had green eyes and wore a brown robe. I was puzzled and with a sense of shock I couldn't help but ask her if "Jesus is my Spirit Guide?"?! The artist chuckled and replied "No. This Guide of yours is named 'Andrew'. He is here to watch over and teach you."

It wasn't until weeks later that I remembered the last experience and description of my Guide in a brown robe with long hair. Anyway, as we progressed into the session, the Medium began to connect with you Kieran . . .

This is what your very first message to me was as told by the lovely Medium as she heard it and as it was taped for me. I had told her nothing about you other than I had just experienced a close loss.
"He is telling me to say "sorry mum". He didn't mean to do it. Spur of the moment thing . . . Stupid . . . at the time there was . . . he was being high—as in a different space mentally . . . should have gone to sleep. He would have been over that feeling.

In particular absolutely nothing to do with you mum, don't feel blame or hurt
It was a silly instant decision . . . Stayed around you until this moment until you came because he knew you needed to know that.

. . . Talking about an Uncle David. Never really thought he would be dead but however finding himself in this space now realises where he has to go and there's others coming around him at this point . . . .

. . . With a big dog. (David once had a big dog named "Bundy".) Sends his love. Understands the hurt. Thank you for the wonderful life you provided for him and it's made it possible for him even now to think in positive terms and move forward.

He is being surrounded to take him forward . . . .
. . . going towards the Light now . . ."I'll be back . . . I will be back."

He is going to do what he needs to do and says he will be there in thought. A Guide is coming around you Alex . . . for comfort . . .
. . . a beautiful moment when he went on . . . extraordinary! . . . very touching."

There was no stopping the tears.

6th August, 2007

This has been a trying week for a variety of reasons. A week ago Bid and I seemed to be in a "turf-war" (!) between two dance schools with emails flying backwards and forwards, both teachers hoping to teach Bridget dance. Bid was in tears and wishing to dance for both. With only three years to go of 15 year training, I did not wish Bridget to give up her current ballet training and I fought hard to keep all parties happy. Finally, with your sister in tears and my own gut churning, I managed after a week of stress to propose a middle ground that allowed Bid to do both. Phew!

Next I had to tackle some financial issues. I just resigned at my Tuesday job at the doctors' surgery after already resigning and then going back. I find that I am having trouble concentrating and think four days a week at my other job is plenty. My new employer is in its sixth week and we still don't know what our hourly rate is. I do know that I'm down financially each week because there is no salary sacrifice with this company. To top it off, work has employed a receptionist and reduced our nursing hours! All in all, my pay is way down. I am filling up the credit cards that I had emptied and hidden, just to pay the bills.

Meantime, back at the ranch, Chris has had oral surgery and requires nursing. He is miserable. It has been hard on Chris at school because the two of you had shared year 10 together at the same school. You both shared some of the same friends and there are a zillion memories that Chris must deal with daily.

I feel exhausted and stumble on through the week – I try to remain cheerful and caring. No one at work would know how much my heart aches . . . or my body for that matter! I worry about my anger towards Aimee and am close to hating her. I know I need to release these negative emotions and consider writing her a letter. It was her birthday recently, her 18th. I didn't want to acknowledge her day. I have already used sage in her room to cleanse it.

Friday night and I'm in tears. A new, previously unseen photo of you Kieran, appeared on the computer, along with a little movie. It showed you cracking your whip, your friends cheering you on. I miss my boy.

Bridget is currently dancing six days a week at present; parent/ teacher interviews are on and mum's taxi is running hot!

Saturday brought a phone call from my mother-in-law. As you well know Kieran, we struggle to understand each other. Both of us have different "truths" and look at things very differently. I deeply wish we could be friends but following a recent incident involving you boys, I considered it best for both of us if we kept our lives on a separate path with the exception of important events. This would allow us each our independent autonomy. However, her need to discuss this with me on Saturday morning (on this week, of all weeks) led to the two of us getting into a tangle of opposite views until I found myself yelling! I never yell at anybody (except you kids!). Well! This moment brought out the worst in me! For 45 minutes we were at it, hammer and tongs. Man, we were going nowhere! We haven't resolved anything and the last of my energy is in tatters and dangling around my feet!

Then the Aimee dilemma – I succumbed in the last hour and shot a quick birthday message by SMS, receiving no acknowledgement. I will, I think, write a letter to the girl whom has deeply hurt and affected every member of our family. Chris declared this morning how much turmoil he feels by his own indecision about sending a card. My advice is to do an action with love and mean it. If you can't, then don't. Chris decided by the end of the day that he has given Aimee opportunities and doesn't wish to send anything. Fair enough. I didn't push him. I feel the same. I am not unaware Kieran, that despite your sister driving you nuts sometimes, you would not like to see the family divided by such ugliness and sadness. However, I cannot imagine a bigger hurt to give someone than deliberately turning your back when one of your own dies. I hope that I will understand Aimee's bad behaviour one day. Not yet though. Nowhere near it.

And so today, it is four months exactly since your accident. My stomach is in knots. Every month on 'anniversary time' it is the same. I can't settle the nausea or palpitations.

Whilst all this was going on, I have spent hours researching the business I have agreed to go into with my new partner. We have had meetings, ideas, solutions, rental agreement discussions. I have been a nurse non-stop for 29 years. I live and breathe nursing – can I really walk away from it?

The last few weeks have been traumatic in arranging the paperwork for your life insurance! How many 17 year old sons sign insurance papers leaving a payment to his family in the event of his death? My anger at God knew no bounds with this arrangement. I cried and begged God to let me exchange payment so we could have you back. "Hey God, please tell me your bank account number at the White Light Banking Corp and I shall pop a wee cheque in for the repurchase of my baby . . . Ebay wasn't developed for nothing . . . PLEASE!!!" This outburst was indeed followed by unsavoury and rather distasteful screeching. You would have heard it from Heaven no doubt. It was Grandma who made me see that these days, insurances are a part of the modern world and to be accepted. It would give you, Kieran, great pleasure she said, to leave us this precious gift.

Speaking of you, my beautiful Kieran, I went to the cemetery on Saturday to tidy up your grave and take fresh flowers. I often sit there and write in this journal. Your Grandpop and Shirley gave me the present of a camp chair to sit on at your gravesite while I write. On this occasion I had my first look at the memorial plaque placed at the foot of your birthday tree. I took photos and asked the tree to grow tall and strong. The plaque stated, "In memory of Kieran Shae Browne on his eighteenth birthday 13.06.07." Again it hit me what a long road ahead I have without you. It is at these moments that I am at my weakest. The reality of your physical absence again sticks in my heart like a knife. With enormous effort I dragged my thoughts back to something kinder and found anything that I could be glad about. Like Pollyanna playing the Glad Game, I dug around desperately to find how glad I am that your tree plaque looks so handsome . . . and so another screaming pear shaped moment was diverted.

I always loved Pollyanna.

With all these items floating around my head, I suppose it wasn't strange that I had a huge hissy-fit tonight when I discovered that

Chris at 16 and Bid at 14, both have their own email addresses. Neither of them asked and Chris declared that he knew what he was doing and had read the conditions, so no problems.

No problems? Bloody kids today want everything, have everything, won't pay for anything, and have rights to everything. I tried to express concern about young people getting in over their heads and having parents be aware of what happens with their kids for the sake of safety, and earning rights to things, etc. Chris told me that "not that you're dumb or anything mum, but you don't understand anything to do with the computer world." RED RAG TO BULL!!

However, the kids would not understand my points of view. "So what's the problem?" The problem is that this technological, cold, insensitive, careless, destructive, superficial, selfish, expensive, wasteful, time-consuming, brain washing world of today is tearing me up.

Trees are cut down, nature slashed, animals destroyed, family life reduced, priorities destroyed, greediness, marketing, selfishness everywhere. My children have been sucked into a life I don't want them to have. I get no choice. They seem arrogant and demanding to me. It is we parents that seem to pay for all those demands (from schools, associations, churches, peers) but these children will never see how privileged they really are.

My heart aches for the loss of simplicity. I have no rights as a parent and I'm getting too tired to care much more. I am tempted to walk away and tell them to buy their own crap and exert all their rights happily without me. If they all know so much, then what the hell am I here for? I am tired and the world cracks some more. This generation will be the death of me . . . or hang on . . . maybe it will be post war generation that deserves their turn that will be the death of me! Interesting to be the first generation of adults to be caught between two completely opposite upbringings – both demanding! And worst of all? This is just another frigging normal week.

Friday, 10th August

Today I felt the need to pull out all your Christmas stories, pictures, paintings and Mother's Day cards. I guess I wanted to be close to you and "hear" from you. What a beautiful child you were, with such a lovely heart. As per your cards, all done in grey lead because of your colour blindness, I can tell you that you didn't need to thank me my darling for doing things for you, but thank you for noticing. Of course I bawled for hours and even into my sleep. I can't remember overnight, but my pillow was soggy and my eyes looked disgusting!

I stopped by at the cemetery on the way home at 5pm while it was getting dark and a blustery storm was brewing. The birds were riled and mucking around, all weird and excitable – rosellas, cockatoos, galahs – so noisy, but lovely to hear. I felt a little closer to you sitting on your chest as I'm prone to doing and maybe that prompted me to dig through the cupboard for evidence of my beautiful son. So I wound up with many tears to match many items. I put aside some items to go to your dad. There was a beautiful photo of your grandad and you at about four-five months. Such a gorgeous child. Found more of you and me too, which was good because I'm usually on the wrong side of the camera for memory shots.

Mum

Saturday, 11th August

I felt miserable and aching today. My very centre was in tatters after grieving all night and crying in my sleep. I was due to go to Langwarrin for a two day course in Reiki Certificate I. I arrived flustered and not particularly in a learning mood! I didn't really want to meet anyone. As usual, I was polite and smiley, then experienced such deep dismay when told by my teacher that only Spirit Guides and Tibetan Higher Teachers were allowed to stay with us. After specifically asking you to come with me Kieran, you were then asked to go. I felt awful . . . plus I didn't want you to go. I did feel nervous, I must admit. Nonetheless, the day progressed well and I learnt so much, not only about Reiki energy and healing, but also about my own abilities and spiritual progress. There were four of us and we soaked it up. Reiki was amazing and increased my ability to channel energy by incredible amounts.

There is so much to learn and practice is imperative. I think nursing helps immensely with being comfortable as a Practitioner. I also experienced colours/auras with my third eye for the first time. I need to figure out the meanings of everything though. By the time I got home, I felt better about myself and a bit closer to the spirit world.

It seems to soothe me to understand that there is a wider picture than our daily view.

Sunday, 12th August

Last night was Bridget's Cabaret and it was quite enjoyable. Bid danced well as she always does.

Today's Reiki was another fascinating event. We learnt to Reiki each other. I began to see more than colours – for example, the picture of an ear appeared in my mind and my 'patient' did suffer ear infections. I also saw aura lines around someone. With Reiki certificate in hand, I discovered that the four of us were once Egyptian Healers (frustrated by politics!) We all had the same Egyptian vision – amazing! You shot me congratulations with my certificate – thank you Kieran. That made me smile. I have another Reiki treatment in a week's time to help me get on my feet and also hopefully chat with you a while. It is my hope that I become practiced enough to hear you myself Kieran, in conversation and not just on rare occasions when I happen to tune in by good fortune. I am continuing to read as much as I can about the Spiritual side of things.

21st August, 2007

Last week I experienced extreme anxiety and felt so teary. I was calmed on Tuesday afternoon by picking up flowers for you Kieran and tidying up your "room" at the cemetery. I also spent one and a half hours sitting on you on Sunday and writing in this journal whilst sipping coffee. I found it very soothing and relaxing. Unfortunately my issue for today involved pain – specifically hip and lower abdomen. The chiropractor didn't help much and pain killers not very useful. I was awake for most of last night and miserable this morning. I really did not wish to go to work this morning and have little interest in nursing anyone. My time as a nurse is winding down I think – my heart is no longer in the game. I'm still a good nurse and provide excellent care, but I don't feel like doing it with spontaneity. I have always said, "If you can't do something with love, then don't do it."

Tonight I went to visit Rene for a Reiki treatment and a Medium catch up, you gorgeous boy. (Please note readers that a Reiki or energy healing and a Medium reading are two different modalities.) You gave Rene a little typical cheek! "Give it to her Rene" you cheeked! Just to remind both of us, your message to me was that you miss me and our cuddles. We had great cuddles for sure. I miss them too.

Interesting to me was Rene's insight into my past life.

Alexandra the Knight Templar gets stabbed by javelin through the left hip and out other side before falling off horse whilst on crusade! That explains a sore hip for sure! I've always been quite uncomfortable with horses!

Also, you feel I keep the barriers up and should let them down a bit. Love the others like I loved you (you mean love you?) and also, I need to cry more. Now I'm confused, because a couple of years ago, you told me not to cry when you are gone. I was trying to be brave and not annoy you, but I guess that does just shove all that aching down deep. I was also reassured that your passing was of your own choosing and timing. Well, as you wish Kieran, but I don't have to bloody well like it. I can just about visualise my bleeding and torn heart.

However, there is some merit in your observation that my other wonderful children may well require more from me. They do not come to me lately with their stuff, nor do we cry together much. Mal tells me that they are cautious with me and do not wish to set off any tears. Apparently the guys talk to him about any issues because it hurts them to see me crying about anything. They cannot bear to see me upset. Since I have never been a weepy person, I guess that makes sense. It also makes things difficult for me. I now feel I should hide myself a bit. Hang on, didn't you say not to hide my feelings Kieran? . . . oh brother . . . ! Now I am more confused. Where is the book called "Grief for Dummies" when you need it?!

I thought since seeing Rene, whom is a Medium, I would try going to have a past life regression session. This is a new thought. I do not really have an opinion on it but it will be interesting to see what it is all about! So much to learn . . .

Sunday, 26th August, 2007

Tough week this one Kieran.

My friend at work went into great detail about her son and his army adventures. I tried to be pleased for them both but I kept seeing you in your uniform (which is hanging on your wardrobe door handle). You picked it up from army disposals. "How do I look mum, in my uniform? Do you think I look alright?" My darling son, you looked superb — so grown up and heading straight for the army! I didn't really want to encourage you and thereby, send you off!

Back at work, whilst I was attending a dressing, my friend continued to detail service life – how much did that hurt! Unable to hear any more, I left the room suddenly and cried for a time in the patients' change room (there were no tissues and I had to grab a paper theatre shoe to wipe my nose!). I wiped my eyes and went back to work. Unfortunately, my broken heart refused to be pushed back into its box and I continued to cry on and off – finally, being discovered by various staff members whom supplied me with cuddles and tissues . . .

I gave up at 11.30am and took the rest of the day off! I went down to the cemetery and sat on you with the sun on my back and listened to the birds. I cried uncontrollably. I eventually phoned Mal, because I started to feel wildly out of control. He popped down from work and gave me a cuddle with a directive to go home to bed. He shared that he was also teary. I did go home, and cried on and off all day. Chris got a lift home and informed me that he too had cried the night before. Wouldn't you know it . . . Billy came home and quietly shared how teary he was too! "I miss Kieran so much . . ." he said. Finally, Bid phoned from ballet class where she had gone straight from school. "Mum, I'm not coping – can you come and get me?" All of us, Kieran, crashed. All devastated at the loss of *you*! How amazing that we all crashed at the same time! Coping is a very exhausting business.

I felt compelled to ring your "other mother" (your ex-girlfriend's mum) Kieran and invite her to lunch on Saturday. Lisa was pleased to hear from me and cried. Lisa and Tara haven't been coping and both needed to hear from me, but didn't want to bother me. Tara begged to see me earlier on, like just after your death, but my understanding was that you and Tara were over back in January. I was drained from coping with everything and everyone and Tara was hysterical. Instead of 'counselling' her, I asked her mum to take her to see someone. I thought you had broken up months before, so I didn't feel the need to encourage close contact with our family. Imagine my shock yesterday, when I found out that you were staying with this family again a couple of weeks before you died!

Kieran, these guys found out about you via MySpace for goodness sakes! If I had known that you and Tara had made up, I would have included her in everything, no wonder the girl is not healing. Although I'll make it clear that I didn't exclude her – I just didn't think to make a special effort to the family, simply because I thought you had left them behind and in your past. I feel simply awful. I drove Lisa down to see your gravesite and your birthday tree and let her cry. Then we went for lunch at the school house and chatted outside in the sun. I think she felt a bit better when I dropped her off, but she was exhausted.

I have promised to send over a few things for Tara. The poor kid – she says you and her were to marry in a few years. You just both needed to grow up a bit. How true, but sad. Did you still love her, son?
Today I was approached by a mum at dance (Bid's jazz exam today!) whom wanted advice/chats on leaving her husband. She lost her brother when she was 16 and seemed to think I'd understand or something. I often wonder why I attract so many people "in trouble."

My ability to cope seems boundless at times and then suddenly, I feel shocked when I crash.

I love you.
Mum

September/October, 2007. Five months.
Not a single day has passed without me thinking of you a thousand times a day. I've been teary the last couple of weeks without realising specifically why really. Does there have to be a why?

Time rolls on quickly and I have many experiences to tell. It is mid October and the past weeks have been strange. I went several weeks ago to a past life reading, but unfortunately, it sparked an unwanted response. It led into my past Indian life as a male leader and Liam again, being my son, but dying. I was arrogant and fought with him, driving him away and ultimately to his death. I heard the area Osaga in my brain and looked this up in my atlas when I got home. It turns out to be an area in the plains of America, near the Mississippi. I had heard 1871 and with curiosity I had later researched the year and Osaga on line and felt amazed that there was even such a place. It was a time of war and atrocity between Native American Indians and the incoming pioneers. I don't know. I didn't like the way the reading went and my very analytical self had found a past that I couldn't fix and instead of soothing me, I felt like I now have two lives of balls up. Rene picks up past lives too from time to time when I'm having Reiki.

Rapes, losses, violence. I'm becoming more and more weary . . .

Although Past Life regression is a new and exciting modality, I do not think I am ready to consider this.

27th October, 2007

There is a full moon tonight – seven months! If anything, the pain seems more acute. It is more settled into a permanent ball of exquisite agony in the centre of my being. I have been irrational, cranky, and deeply ill at ease with myself and easily irritated for the last couple of months. This has been superimposed with the cover up emotions. I am easily loved by my patients – known as caring, ever helpful, supportive and hugely cheeky. My patients laugh under my care, which fits in with a generally happy unit despite the emotional turmoil of patient amputations and pain. The patients chatter on, unaware of my own turmoil. I knew a full moon was on its way because the world itself has been cranky this week. Ask any nurse or doctor and they will tell you how strange people become when there is a full moon. Add the pain of my baby leaving for the Spirit world on the night of a huge red full moon and I am forever attached to the months and lunar cycles.

I have been sitting on your gravesite Kieran, crossed legged and bawling again. Actually, I always think of it as . . . sitting on your chest. Remember how we could cuddle up at anytime Kieran. If you were lying on your bed, I would just shove you and you would move over making room for me and throwing your arm over me. Or in the lounge chair, we would sneak closer. As I'm lucky enough to see in a photo, you would stretch out, putting your head in my lap and allow me to play with your dark, thick wavy hair.

As for my misery back in the Berwick cemetery . . .

The sun shone on my shoulders as I fiddled with the dirt, plucked a few shreds of grass that were slowly enveloping the edges of your plot and fluffed up the new flowers I'd just placed at the edges of your site, all in quick succession. I closed my eyes and let the sun sink into my skin. The ache and the sobs that escaped me, pumped in unison until gradually the episode began to subside. As I quieted, I began to feel the peace of the cemetery. There is a lot of love in this place of losses. Powerful and peaceful 'sunrays' began to flood into me from above. Orange and yellow circles buzzed around my consciousness. Initially, I was just focusing on relaxing and becoming calm. Before I closed my eyes, the words at the bottom of your plaque jumped out at me. . . . Not gone from us, just gone before us . . . and the word *'remember'* echoed around my head. I relaxed more and thought suddenly that these sunrays are gifts of love and healing from the Spirit world. The thought was so right, so fitting.

As my awareness zoned in and out, occasional thoughts of mine shot out and thoughts shot back at me which I don't think were mine! "Kieran, I miss you . . . oh God" shot out and then quickly before I even had time to form another thought, you shot back, "I'm here . . ." then . . ."I promised . . ." and I knew the rest of the sentence would be, "I promised to never leave you." The deep knowledge that you were with me, your arm around my shoulders was so calming. I knew, just knew you were beside me, although damn it, I couldn't see you. Peace and love still poured into my being. Suddenly, at the same time that I casually wondered at what time it was, I heard/felt the word, "go." My awareness abruptly but nicely returned. I took a moment to orientate myself and sent a prayer of love and thanks before I lifted myself off the ground and made my way towards the car. I climbed in and looked at the car clock – 1.55pm. I had five minutes to make it to my hairdresser's appointment! I felt calm, serene and loved. I just (again) knew that all the lights would be green. All week, every darn set off traffic lights went red at my approach – I've been cranky all week . . . Just as I approached a newly turned red light, a voice said "turn", so left I went, a different way. Oh a green light, then another . . . oh . . . arrival on time and all green lights! Beautiful Spirits, you really do look after me. Thank you Kieran, I will endeavour to remember.

The following Saturday I popped in again for 10 minutes during the week to say hi to you before meeting Liam in Berwick. We have been having a lot of coffees together of late and he shares his life with me. He hurts so badly and misses you so much. I wish he wouldn't be so darn full on 'Christian' though because I feel it blocks his opportunities to connect to you. Rene offered to do a reading for him so he could talk to you, but that made him angry. I would hate to deal with straight grief without being able to contact you. It would quite literally kill me not to have the ability to connect to you Kieran. Hearing your voice and receiving your messages enables me to get out of bed in the morning.

These last six weeks have been an incredible journey. After the last past-life regression, I became a bit angry, cranky . . . One day (you will remember this Kieran) I lost the plot and experienced the most outrageous anger. I wanted to die. Then again, I was angry that my soul wouldn't die . . . endless churning – just like Groundhog Day! The Christian concept of one life and one Heavenly reunion is simpler and kinder I think. However, I have slowly developed the more Buddhist type understanding over the last few years. Keep coming back and doing it again until the lesson is learnt. Man, I'm so tired! But unfortunately for me, I believe that this is how it is and how God plans it all. All religions pray to the same God. Simple. People make it messy and complicated.

So there I was, wanting to run myself off the road, hating everything and everyone. Reckless driving, endangering everyone. I didn't care. Suddenly, I felt cold air on my hands. I had the heater on! Then the same thing happened again. I checked the dials – heaters on. More cold air. "Hello" I said to my angry self, someone is here with me. No, I'm too angry. Go away. With that, I continued on my grumpy way. I punched the radio on, and it began to play. But no, Kieran you had other ideas. The radio turned itself off abruptly. The CD player began to work. Amazingly, the CDs popped in and started a song then popped out. I angrily declared to the Spirit World that I didn't care and continued tearing around corners and slamming my car angrily down streets. My rage was huge. The CD began to pop in and out faster and faster. The thought gradually dawned on me that I was worrying you and you were frantically sending me messages. It took another couple of streets to start calming down and when I finally arrived in the work car park, I was shaking and in need of a cry. Unluckily for me, we had a lot of patients already arrived and the noise of the early morning chatter filled the building. I wished I could go home.

As I stepped into the room, the bathroom buzzer went off and Liz told me that the buzzers had been going off and no-one was in the bathroom! She had already turned off a couple. Sure enough, when I checked, no-one was there. Yet another miracle came my way straight after that. One of the patients' wives caught my eye amongst the crowded room and motioned for me to come to her. As I stepped toward her, she came to her feet, out of her chair and across to me. She wasn't smiling. Solemnly, she took my hand and curled my fingers around something she dropped into my palm. With concern in her eyes, she told me that the rose quartz crystal heart on a chain she had just given me would calm and relax me. How the hell did she know I needed it right now? I took a deep breath and let the moment lead me. I'm sorry I'm so grumpy Kieran. I had said a positive Mantra just that morning and still got engulfed in negativity. I don't understand this thing called grief. It rolls along doing whatever it pleases. I have so much to learn.

Just this week, I went to see Rene. I feel so achy and grumpy. I decided I needed to tap in and chat to you, sunshine. Plus, I doubted that you are speaking to me or that I have been hearing you. So I went for a quick Reiki and a quick talk. The night before, I had wandered into your room and asked you if Bid could take your camping gear away to camp. Then I asked Liam if he would like to look after your camping stuff when it was returned. He sounded quite pleased to accept.

Next day at Rene's, the first thing she told me was that you had popped into her class looking for me! "She's not here yet Kieran", you were told. The next thing she told me was, "You have to do something about the room Alex. He's telling me that you should give away his stuff so it can be used." Rene couldn't have known that I went in and collected some gear. So, okay Kieran, gradually, I shall clean up your room and filter out your bits and pieces to where you want them to go. You also told me your work in Heaven is way more important than your work here. I understood that you are telling me not to grieve, but rather accept that you are needed. I asked for confirmation that I was receiving your messages. You told me, "You are not listening . . ." I felt quite indignant right then because I'm trying to understand and I'm not all that smart you know!

Slowly, over the next couple of days, I began to see that yes, you are with me and have kept your promise. The messages are clear enough – Rene also told me, that yes, I do hear you and I shouldn't doubt. She also said to look out for a confirmation message from you.

. . ."It's something nice, and this time *don't doubt it!*"

Well, I've looked out for a few days now, not knowing what I'm looking for!

On the way home from work on Friday, it was lightly raining. I was driving home and thinking of you. I recalled that I hadn't as yet identified a message. I spoke to you out loud – "Gee Kieran, I hope I don't miss your message. Make sure it is really obvious. You know how hopeless I am." I sat at the red light then began to turn the corner. There in front of me, suddenly and brightly, lay the hugest and most beautiful rainbow ever! Man, it was *huge* and complete!

Often you see a half rainbow. This one was beautiful. I squealed with delight . . ."Kieran, did you send me a rainbow? Thank you, it's lovely." Something nice and *don't doubt it.*" Okay son. It's a great gift of confirmation. Thank you darling. The bonus was understanding that you are often around watching over us.

The other recent gift from you was a massive one. It was a gift for my birthday, and *I loved it.* Mal had arranged a dozen coloured helium filled balloons for my 46th birthday. Each of them defiantly declared '21' on them. I concur! The balloons were huddled over the dining table in the dining room. However, one stubborn balloon had a mind of its own. It kept wandering off. It startled Bridget by following her to the laundry. Then it inched its way to the lounge room and sat quietly on the lounge suite – where you sit actually. Each time, one of us collected it and returned it to the dining room.

Next day, I found the same balloon floating in your bedroom. I was a bit slow on this occasion, I must admit. I spoke to the balloon and asked it where it thought it was going. I returned it to the collective. However, to some degree of amusement and exasperation on your behalf I imagine, the balloon began to move down past the kitchen and into the lounge. It moved past three of us and stopped to peek in at Bridget's room. We stood stunned and silent watching. One of us stood at the front door, hand on the knob and door half open. Air whistled in. I broke the silence saying out loud, "The door is open and it's windy. It must be pushing the balloon in." Bid looked at me, then the balloon. Patiently, she informed me "Mum, the wind is blowing in this way but . . . the balloon is going *that* way!" and pointing in the opposite direction. Sure enough, the balloon continued on past Bid's room, into my room. We all followed. It pottered into my bedroom, across the bed and nestled into my 'V' pillow. I broke the silence with a laugh and called out my thanks to you Kieran. That was great!

Over the next few days, I would move the balloon at night and find it at my feet in the morning. Knowing you were there each day was so soothing. Thank you!

7th November, 2007

I started a Trans-healing course tonight, to allow me to learn about aura fields, chakras, energy healing and a whole heap more. We began work learning how to protect ourselves with white light and other processes. It was a little more nerve wracking because I felt so naive and perhaps even too ignorant to be allowed in. However, I boldly decided that even if I understood only 50 per cent of the work, then that's 50 per cent more knowledge than I had before!

We also focused on how to learn about our own bodies and minds with a meditation – "How is the weather in there?" Inside my body, there is constant sad drizzle. My throat, solar plexus and stomach are dark coloured with ongoing rain. My heart is shattered and lies in black pieces somewhere in my pelvis, which aches. Visualising a happy inside to promote health and love is important. Tonight's outcomes are important and positive but I'm tired. I discussed my findings with the Teacher, my long suffering Spirit Guide. I asked for help in my journey for inner peace. Losing a child in this life is the ultimate in pain and I will need to learn to gain insight and clarity from this extreme challenge. I know you are okay Kieran and watching over us and therefore the pain is more mine than yours. I will try hard to learn how to smile and love again to make you proud. I seem to have deep anger however – this will be a tough journey.

9th November, 2007

Seven months exactly by lunar time Kieran. Liam finally cried for hours today . . . Thank God – he was so grumpy yesterday. He misses you so much. He curled in his bed this afternoon for a couple of hours after feeling abashed for crying in front of Marilyn. They have been going out for a few months now. You were of course right Kieran; he did have someone waiting for him!

I managed to keep busy all day at work and into the night, largely due to Pauline and I shopping for her wedding next weekend. But I didn't forget for a second! Oh, no siree! Seven months of Hell on Earth. How I miss you Kieran.

17th November, 2007
Seven months by dates of you living back at home in the Spirit world and . . . Wedding day for Pauline and Terry.

This has been a tiring week – I cried Tuesday all morning, then again at night and several times since. I feel consumed by guilt all the time. The more I process your going Kieran, the more I find something to berate myself over. I remember events, moments and flashbacks to moments in time when I could have or should have . . . was I a good mum Kieran? I wish I could have been a better mum. I wish I could think of happy memories and profound mothering examples of saving the day! The image of being a perfect, calm and loving cheery and stress-free mother bearing down to rescue the children from the world with a serene smile and giant hugs . . .

I remember myself rushing, yelling, half-hearing and missing opportunities to catch up with you. You gave me openings to share with you, to find out what was profound and important in your life. Talking about your impending death . . . God, Kieran, this one area of omission on my behalf will anchor itself to my soul and heart forever. The pain of regret is truly massive. And so I have cried a lot.

My second Trans-healing class proved to be very difficult also. I think I tend to block a lot of my spiritual side because it hurts to still my mind. Stopping to meditate and step into spiritual matters leaves me wide open for *pain*!

So . . . trying to learn about spiritual matters without practicing is a bit tricky . . . apart from that, I don't actually understand the whole thing! It's all about auras, chakras and things I can't remember, all with long-winded names. And only eight weeks to go! I found out that I'll be able to feel the energies better once the letting go of grief is over. Humph. Well, I miss you and I know you miss me so then, I have no desire to let go. I am trying not to just call you all the time though. I'm told you have work to do (and you told me yourself that your role is much more important now than before . . .). I feel a bit frustrated at my lack of understanding. I have developed a new awareness of the complexities of the Spirit World, learning how much I don't know! Be patient with me son! I suppose you are right again, because I don't listen to you well enough – how can I when I block my own meditations? Well now, this is going to be a long learning curve Kieran!

And so it was that Mal and I found ourselves on this special wedding Saturday at lunch-time, in the cemetery remembering seven months journey. Both of us bawling, missing you. Once my heart is out, I can't seem to rein it in. Of course, then going to Pauline's wedding proved to be a challenge. Our hearts ached. Pauline and Terry were married in the vineyard. Chris, Liam, Marilyn and I stood and watched from under the tree while Mal was camera man. Pauline looked stunning. Both Lisa and Carol were beautiful. It was a lovely wedding. I feel sure somehow that you were with us.

I was delighted to share this wonderful event . . . but I'm afraid that I became unhitched on the last song! "The Wedding Song"— . . ."when a man leaves his mother and a woman leaves her home" . . . Oh my . . . I had been crying over my lost son all day and felt the loss of never seeing him marry right then. *Tears*! I tried to run away but was noticed. However I was really, truly happy for Pauline and Terry. They both deserve every minute of happiness.

It was difficult to continue on into the night's festivities with swollen eyes and aching head, not to mention heart. However, it was a lovely event, wasn't it?

21st November, 2007
Meantime, on Sunday, I took a call from Kingi whom we raced over to arrange an ambulance for. He is now in CCU with unstable angina for the third night in a row. I asked God to bless Kingi with improved health and keep him here with us for a long time yet.

PS: I just remembered an event at the wedding . . . Mal was chatting to a gentleman next to him and was asked how many kids he has. Mal answered, "five" which is what we tend to say. Anyway, the gent laughed and said to Mal – "Oh, well you can afford to lose one then . . . !

Oh, not funny . . . *so* not funny!

28th November, 2007
Kieran, today it's your Uncle Harry's birthday. He is 50! And he is away at sea where we can't badger him. That's cheating big brother! Kingi is also better and back home.

So we reach another diary, precious son of mine. Yesterday, and indeed this week, has been difficult. Of course everything is made worse by me stopping my fibromyalgia medication. My nerve endings are screaming at me! Actually, I didn't stop the meds, I just ran out. With Bid doing rehearsals every day, running around and organising all her dozen costumes and accessories, dropping off and picking up Chris, along with work each day . . . time is a premium we don't have.

Mum and her partner Pat are flying down tomorrow night from Queensland to see Bid in her four concerts over the weekend. It will be lovely to see them. Mal has been racing to paint Aimee's old room which I have had to 'bless' often and ask for help cleaning out Aimee's negative vibes. I tried yesterday to Reiki her bed, but man, you should have seen the dark red angry colours that rushed like fire before my Third Eye. I hope I protected myself enough from the negativity of it all. Maybe I should arrange my own Reiki treatment. That girl is so angry and bitter. I have to say that I'm glad she is no longer with us, only because she refuses to learn love with us. I hope and pray she might learn it somewhere else. We have had to put Aimee on the back burner. We still feel so much ache over the entire problem.

Anyway, back to the issues at hand. Mal and I have busted ourselves to fix up 'mum's' room, clean the house, pick up groceries and clear up the back yard. The back garden looks beautiful – tan bark replaced and new plants in. Gorgeous!

So then, what's eating me?

Kieran, your insurance cheque arrived today. I don't know how to thank you, or be so grateful, or even, how to process this. It's been seven months and each day is hard and painful. Every day when I wake, remembering is a whole new death. If I could give God this cheque and say, "Please, may I exchange this for my son's return?" it would solve all my problems. Hey God, I've learnt heaps from this experience so, how's about you shoot Kieran back to me now, huh? Thanks for the lessons – I'll be sure to pass them on, okay?

I do hear from you Kieran, fairly often and also the Teacher, my Spirit Guide, but I'm such a novice at spiritual things that I think

I mix you both up quite often. I think I may also have mother/son conversations on my own too! Sometimes though, when I hear your words Kieran, then answer, my mind doesn't have time to formulate the next response but I know I hear words so in my ignorance, but also in Faith, I assume it is you answering. I tested this recently – My friend "see's folk" and recently whilst visiting her, she told me that I brought someone with me and I had in fact just been having mental conversations with you. So cool! Helps me heaps with my healing and coping. Thank you for being there for me. As for leaving us with insurance money . . . oh Lord.

5th December, 2007

I dropped my Mum and Pat at the airport yesterday. We enjoyed a wonderful five days. They fitted in and did their own thing. We also visited a few local areas and had coffees out every day! Your Grandma visited you at the cemetery twice. She climbed back in the car with her eyes full of tears after spending a quiet time with you. I showed her your tree which incidentally has grown way taller than me. It is a Flowering Gum so will be huge.

I phoned the cemetery management about securing the burial site across from you but it appears I can't. I am allowed to purchase one a couple up from your tree but not on the lawn with you. Since I don't know who might wish to jump in, it's difficult to estimate how many places with our extended family may be needed or more precisely, wanted. There are two places with you Kieran, but I figured our tiny cemetery will be full in 20 years and you are not staying in there by yourself, so don't argue. If I buy one more plot nearby yours, that secures a few spots for somebody in the future. Makes me feel better. Funny how I can toss these issues around without a drama. I also got distracted because I was saying that Grandma's visit was an especially pleasant one!

Whilst here, Grandma and Pat went with us to Bridget's performance of Thumbelina. She danced beautifully and managed her role of Swallow with magnificence. She was a hip hop swallow with attitude and really stood out, didn't she? Many positive comments came back. I'm very proud of her. However, I have changed noticeably in my personality. I get so easily anxious these days. I was beside myself with worry about Bid and her quick changes. I seem to worry more and feel anxiety like I have never felt before. I've always been calm with problems and just plough through them with minimal drama. Now though, I really experience high anxiety easily. I worry incessantly about you children.

I have experience with grief but it has long been practiced at work. I do not know how to tell if my kids are okay with their grieving process or in their general lives. The entire business keeps my gut tangled. What is "normal" when it comes to grief? Do adults and children grieve the same? Are there hidden symptoms I should be aware of with teenagers? Maybe all weird behaviour is acceptable. What if I'm not noticing that my children are not coping? How long does this whole business go on for? I can't find anything to read that tells me that none of us are losing our minds . . . or that we are! Okay, turn it all off . . .

Liam wants to purchase a car. This sounds nice and normal at least! You will have seen it and probably been green with jealousy! You know that a sports car mixed with your enthusiasm would have been a cocktail of mischief! I hope Liam's Spirit Guides are on the ball. I do not wish to arrange any more funerals.

Liam's birthday is next – we will organise a barbeque for him. Something simple. I know you'll be there. Talk to you soon honey. I love you,
Mum.

6th December, 2007 – eight months today since your accident. Hey Kieran! (I hear you answer "hey mama.") I'm writing from work. I am starting to question my own wisdom over a decision made last week. As a Hyperbaric nurse, I was asked to accompany our team to a conference on hyperbaric history at the Alfred next week. I was busy with mum's visit and just said yes, no problems. But I realise now that things are slowing down, and that I will be going back to a place I haven't seen since I was last "looking after you." You were in the trauma ward with ICU nurses and we will be going to the Hyperbaric Unit (run by ICU nurses). It should be okay, but I'm uncertain of my reactions. When a workmate was admitted to the Alfred, I couldn't make myself go and visit. By the same token I don't want to talk myself into an issue. I need to think positive thoughts and maybe go and see Dr Meagan. I really want to give her a hug. Maybe I will phone Alfred HBU and enquire about what I'll be exposed to. It should be okay.

Karen and Kingi are going to New Zealand tomorrow for Karen's 50th birthday. When they get back, we will be going. I want to try and pick a copy of your neck carving. I dreamt you and I were talking over a tattoo I had in New Zealand. I woke thinking that you would like me to get a tattoo for you. Somehow that thought stays with me. A bit strange, considering I have steadfastly declined any interest in the past. I have always found tattoos undesirable. When Mal had a Ta Moko (traditional Maori tattoo) done, it seemed a great idea. Just not for me! I'm not certain now. Hmmm. Keep convincing me boy, and we'll see.

I hope you will be coming with us to New Zealand. I'm afraid I'm not up to a Melbourne Christmas without you. We are all running away to New Zealand to keep busy, look around, do something memorial for you and of course, see Pop! Pack your bags son!

I had a vision. I was not asleep but I was settling in to sleep. Without warning, I saw two wolves dart out from trees and edge around a fire place. They crept towards a tipi. The tipi merged into the forefront of my sight. (All of this in grainy grey colours.) The tipi receded and in its place a head and shoulders of a senior Indian gentleman appeared. He was grey haired, long hair flowing over his shoulders with several feathers tucked into the back of his long hair. He had a craggy and lined face and he was looking into my eyes. Then, two words were spoken into my ear from elsewhere. "Grandfather" . . . followed by a hesitation . . . then . . ."Kieran." Grandfather Kieran? My Kieran was my grandfather sometime past? It was all out of my control, then gone. I know I wasn't asleep.

13th December, 2007

The 9th December was a teary eight month reminder. I'm learning that it will never be any easier. The day before, I tried cleaning out your clothes and cried the whole time. I don't want to be parted from your belongings, so I put most of them back! I thought I could surely remove your boxers and holey socks but even that became impossible. In fact, it was worse because they were intimate apparel belonging to you. I decided in the end to tidy but not chuck things out. I could hardly see for tears anyway!

Some memories are shoved at you and some arise unbidden. For months I have turned my head away from certain places that were your last contacts. My heart tears at me whenever I drive past the Government Apprenticeship building. Here you were studying your Boiler Making trade. It was exciting to see how you enjoyed beginning your dreams and finally shaking off your school years.

You really did hate being a school student. It was difficult for you at school all your life because you didn't quite fit there. Not only did you struggle with colour blindness and mild deafness, but you also had an incredible sense of black and white justice. There were no shades of grey for you and therefore you developed your own code of honour that was not always consistent with the rules of society.

You were awkward as a pre teen and bewildered easily by life. You saw things from a perspective that even I rarely understood until much later on. I know how much you struggled with academics and rules Kieran. You got behind in school work and were too uncoordinated in sports. You began to feel angry and frustrated. When you were about 12 years old a Child Psychologist finally diagnosed you with mild Autism and Specific Learning Disability. It gave us something to work with in enabling you to be given strategies in coping with others. This now has me shaking my head with disgust at my own ignorance. I think that I didn't understand you were simply you . . . and that you had a strong sense of connection with the Other Side.

Overall though, it was a turning point for you Kieran because we repeated you at school. This was when you realised that you were tall and powerful. Smaller kids followed you like a god. For the first time you found out about power. From this point on your sense of extreme justice, your strength and the underlying anger made for an interesting mix. You became interested in gangs and other social groups. In a few more years you would wind up mucking around with drugs.

I think about the speech therapists, the occupational therapists, the counsellors, the tutors. Did I take wrong turns in my decisions as a mum?

My thoughts continue in a sabotaging sort of way and the days roll on.

I get annoyed that things tug me away from you. For several days now, I've planned to pop into the cemetery to water the flowers but time has run away (mostly from work, as usual . . .).

Last night, Liam had a barbeque for his 22nd birthday. I'm sure you were there. Do you like his new car? A black and white Nissan 180sx with turbo. He picked it up and drove his mates up and down. Kieran, we shall have to watch your brother's back with this car. We want him safe on the road. He tore off down the road in the middle of the night and I heard him down the end of Pound Road, turbo charging. Oh my God, my heart was thudding with fear. I remember saying to Liam about you, "I have to let him go to make his own choices. I have taught him everything I can about being careful." And then you were gone.

Now I have to say the same thing of Liam. How scary is that?!

Incidentally, just now, I decided not to go to the Alfred this afternoon. It makes me feel sick and teary thinking about it all. I'm not ready just yet. Next time.

PS: just heard via Chris that Aimee is pregnant. Mal is beside himself.

25th December, 2007
Another first to get through . . .

Christmas Day. We are in New Zealand having rolled into Wellington on the 19th. We took a spin into the city and up the hill in the cable car – thinking of you Kieran as always. You love new places. We drove up north to Wanganui for a four day stay. None of us wanted Christmas and the tension was building up. Determined not to cry about how much we miss you, we bravely ambled on sightseeing and shopping for Christmas. The same Christmas we were trying to avoid!

A day spent in the jet boat, bush walk, two hour canoeing down the rapids type adventure exhausted and exhilarated us all. Yes,

Kieran, Bid and I canoed downstream for two hours solid in a bulky Canadian canoe! Wonderful, we are, especially since we went down the rapids backwards! My God, Kieran, you would have enjoyed the whole thing so much. I really hope you shared this with us.

The drive from Wanganui to Taupo was uneventful and pleasant. The build up of pre-Christmas tension was growing however. I felt teary on and off, and the guys were grizzly. We arrived at Pops in Taupo late afternoon, rushed to our Batch to unpack and shot off to Taupo shops to try and do last minute shopping for Christmas. Oh Kieran, my heart was heavy and aching. On the drive up, I kept seeing you with all of your bouncing enthusiasm at various places from our last trip. I wanted to stop at some of them but the rush was on and the kids were getting anxious. My heart just bled a little more as we rushed past.

Christmas Day. We all looked so worn and drawn. The dreaded day arrived without our beloved Kieran. I actually feel quite dizzy as I write this, and the emotions swirl around. We all trudged over to your Pops. Bid was the only recipient of Santa and she didn't even open her parcel.

Shirley had several members of her family present and she with Pop had worked so hard for days to prepare a lovely Christmas Day. Liam approached me saying he didn't want to go. We all felt sick and so fatigued! We put on our "we can do this" faces and did the best we could. The meal and the company were lovely, but the five of us were quiet. We had actually hoped that by being here we would avoid having a Christmas but somehow we were misunderstood and we were instead confronted by a huge Christmas! By mid-afternoon we all looked sick and the kids took themselves home for a sleep. Another hour later after helping to clean up, Mal and I joined them. I found Liam on his bed sobbing with grief and battling with severe sinusitis. He was so miserable. I cried a little with him.

We trudged back to Shirley's and Pops for Christmas tea, exhausted. It was a little easier this time with some of the tension lifted. Shirley's son David was bright and bouncy, promising to take the guys out skeet shooting before we left. At last, we filtered home to crash into bed. Christmas Day, over.

I knew it would be hard, but I didn't get how hard until it was upon us. We made it though! I feel that you were there with us from time to time. Not quite the same love, I'm sorry.
Mum

2nd January, 2008

The rest of the holiday to New Zealand was kept busy and it rolled along pretty fast. Taupo Quads, skeet shooting, Rotorua trout farms, Luge course, then finally, Auckland. Liam continued to be ill and we all struggled some days. Home again by 30th December, 2007. Liam cancelled most of his New Year's stuff due to illness but Bid and Chris went out and had some fun.

I went down to see you at the cemetery with Mal on New Year's Eve. Karen and Kingi had maintained the cemetery vigil whilst we were away, taking down flowers and we went a few days later. It had been a hot, hot day and I chose a late visit hoping the cooler weather would settle in.

Oh Kieran, I didn't want New Year. It felt like we were leaving you behind. Now I have to say, "My son died last year", instead of this year. I resent time and all its implications. I cried and cried on your grave. I hate this whole thing. *Hate it*! You are my baby and you should be with us.

9th January, 2008

Nine months today kiddo. I marvel at how we have survived. Then again, what are the damn choices? Still want to lie down and give up often, but there are young adults in my home that need love and support. They all hurt too. Liam is still sick and I worry about him.

Yesterday I took Nat, Bid and Nat's boyfriend James down to the cemetery. The girls cried, especially Natalie. I sat at your tree and cried too. Nine months – that's exactly how long it took me to grow you – to the day, because you arrived exactly on your predicted arrival date. I cry a lot these days, always about you. I can't help it and I don't very often try and stop it. What for? It doesn't change anything whether you cry or not!

By the way, I decided not to go to Daniel's and Tash's Engagement party. I felt that I would make some people uncomfortable as a tragedy reminder and take away some of the joy. I sent flowers of congratulations instead.

20th January, 2008

I don't feel any better since my last entry Kieran. I'm not sure what's going on with me right now, but my grief is deeply imbedded into my chest and stomach – a large, dark and grizzly ball of turmoil and withheld tears that toss about in a sea of pain. It never, ever leaves me, despite the fact that I function quite well on all fronts. My patients don't seem to notice anything amiss, except the occasional, "you look tired today." I generally remain efficient and organised with good humour thrown in for good measure, in generous amounts.

At home, we laugh, we cuddle, we tease. I think the home-front is calm for the most part and Kieran, we all are quite gentle and loving with each other. Since you left, we cuddle and support more and our teasing is gentler. You taught us that I think.

There is a lot on my mind presently too. I have been worrying about Liam's health, Bid at another new school, my new business venture, my current job and its exhausting extension of expectations and work hours. Thursdays are again a 10 hour day without a single break. Life is busy and time gallops on.

The writing of this journal has had some interesting twists in intent. Originally, I started writing this journal so I could discuss this entire situation of loss with you. Well, that hasn't changed, but after a while, I began to see the value of writing as a healing tool. Then Colin my lovely Grief Counsellor, introduced the thought of publishing this journey of grief. This developed the thought as a log to see how much spiritual growth I might make from the moment of loss, through the months to whenever I stop scribbling.

Today, I had the thought that if anyone were to read my idle chitchat to my ascended son, they would be quite bored. Why? Because the theme doesn't change. Heartache ongoing. I have learnt that the pain of loss becomes a part of one's soul. It will never get better and in between my moments of deep grief and the regrets that surface, I am forced to continue my life the best that I can.

My grief of course, encompasses Aimee in all sorts of ways. I feel great pain that I failed to reach Aimee and reverse her destructive ways. Somehow, I think I need to overcome the great hurt I feel about the way she treated us. Feeling compassion for her is a bit of a stretch for my damaged trust, but neither do I want anything horrid to happen to her. Grieving for two kids at once is thirsty work . . .

Kieran, you know already that I visited a Medium again recently hoping, but not expecting a visit from you. This different Medium didn't impress me and I didn't hear from you. However, she did tell me that I had a visit from my dad's father and described him along with his manner. Later, when I asked your Pop, he confirmed my Grandad. The message Grandad gave me was that he was supporting me and, "never doubt that I'm a good mum" which was helpful because I've been beating myself up about the things I didn't do well as your mum.

Trying to get Aimee sorted out took me away from you just as we were getting really close, you and I Kieran. I am so angry at Aimee for stealing precious time from us. I feel like I wasted time on her for nothing since neither of you benefitted. So Grandad chided me for my guilt! Perhaps I would feel different if, at the very least, Aimee gained something from the time I took eyes off you onto her.

As for my spiritual growth, I am not learning at present. I'm struggling to just live with work, the house, three kids and their hobbies and now the "renovating" that we've started again. I stopped studying for a while because it hurt trying to balance grief and understanding spirituality . . . what an emotional juggle!

Spiritually understanding a concept of loss versus the emotion of loss processing is at opposite ends of the same spectrum. I'm not that clever! Needless to say, I'm not at all connected to the Other Side or anything spiritual at present. It's my hope that I develop my soul again soon. I will, because I miss you. You are such a huge piece of me. Surviving without contact to you is not an option. So, I will "see" you soon my friend!

Love, mum xoxo

9th February, 2008

I'm again, sitting on your chest Kieran, at 3pm and it's coldish and a bit blowy. So is my nose for that matter! I'm sobbing my little heart out over your sunflowers and proteas. Actually, the sunflowers are pretty cool – bright and cheery. I hope you like them. It is your, "10-months-of-missing-Kieran-day" today. "How the devil have we managed to survive 10 whole months?" I think, looking back, the acceptance has slowly seeped in, because I've stopped saying every 10 minutes "Fuck, this can't be happening!" Now I only say it sometimes . . . Face it Kieran, it's probably the strongest thing I can think of to say, so I suppose I would never be a candidate for a sailor's certificate!

However, I do realise that I am more frail then ever . . . tearier when I have never been a person to cry. I feel more delicate, more "shatter-able." I still have permanent pain in my chest and my gut still clenches with shock and pain when I think of details or a trigger from elsewhere invades. But something has shifted in my own loss process. I'm guessing that maybe the shock of your "moving out" (shall we call it?), is receding a little with therefore, some acceptance attached. Without the shock battle, there is now just grief. Pain. All on its own. Stark, naked pain. I hate it. I want my son back. You. Come on Kieran, how about jumping out from behind a tree and yelling, "Got ya!"? Hey, I'd laugh, I promise . . . but no, I have a permanent seat here in Berwick cemetery instead.

I have sat and told you my worries – how the family is and how fragile they are too, about Bridget's new school, her dancing, Aimee's baby and all the things you are not to miss out on. I know you check in on us. I regularly have the feeling that you are watching over us and once recently in the evening I was positive you were in the house, but I couldn't pinpoint where. I was so sure that I kept looking around. Suddenly, I flicked my head inexplicably to the left just in time to see an amazing black blur flash across the hall into the dining room – much too fast for a human form. I grinned! Caught you Kieran!

Forgot to tell you that Aimee sent Mal an SMS telling him of her engagement. Good grief! What next?

I spent a couple of hours with Tara's mum Lisa last weekend. She was in tears having a "Kieran moment." She loves you and so does Tara. They miss you. It was nice to have company while we visited in the cemetery – someone to cry with who really understands.

I don't get people checking on us very much. I next to never have friends asking how I'm going, but then I've learnt that losing a child is everyone's very worst nightmare and getting in touch with us causes people pain. Not long ago, I was attempting to tell my GP how I was coping, but she began to cry. She's a mum. So we don't lean on others. Only a couple of times have I attempted small off-loads to friends. If I needed people though, I'm sure we would be supported – it's just that I'm aware how hard it is for the supportee's!

Counsellors are there for a reason. It helps too, because my kids hate seeing me upset. Bid cries when she sees my distress. Bless her socks!

Oh hey! I caught sight of a beautiful rainbow a little while ago! You sent me a gift! Kieran, I saw half of it from the family room window, then in my right ear I heard you say, "It's for you mum". A moment later I heard, "Look at it outside" so I went outside. Sure enough was the other end – a complete rainbow! Thank you honey. You are so special, my precious one. Thank you, especially today.

It helps so much to know you are watching over us or with us. I know I have some degree of clairaudience, but I'm greedy because I wish I could see you as well. Maybe I can develop these skills with work.

15th February, 2008
I'm grumpy, grumpy, grumpy! I worked 11 hours yesterday, long hours, rushing around after patients and I'm sick of the politics . . . yada, yada, problems, fatigue, blah, blah . . . I just seemed to be on the wrong end of everyone's mood today which exacerbated my own grump even more.

Well, I lasted to 6pm, then tears . . . oh floods of them. My grief floweth over . . . When I'm tired, I can't keep my Kieran pain in its neat, tidy box. Funny though, Liam had the same sort of day. Weird how that happens.

The day before yesterday Kieran, I had a sudden flash vision of a courtroom – there and gone. Then a strong feeling that a letter would arrive soon in regards to Daniel's court case. In keeping in touch with the Police, we have learnt that there is still an investigation under way with not much else to tell at present.

Easter is early this year – only a few weeks away. Another first that we rather hope to get through any way we can. No eggs for us.

9th March, 2008

The last few weeks have been difficult as always, but a bit different also. The letter for court didn't appear. That's disconcerting!

I saw, felt and ached over the new moon about 10 days ago. 11 months then and 11 months today also. Forever I will ache and shed tears for you, twice per occasion . . . Mal and I sat up at the cemetery this evening as the sun began to set. We watched those birds bickering again, and sprayed the aphids off your roses.

Yesterday, instead of visiting you at the cemetery, I enjoyed a visit from your mates, Mick and Kim. Kim just got her licence this week and shared with me her dream with you in it. She felt it as a strong message. I told her that you have been seen and heard around a lot, and that you have been explained to me as an Earth Angel. I often get little SMS messages or quick moments of sharing from those that knew you.

Mick told me that he and Kim are going to Tasmania next weekend for Daniel and Tasha's wedding. I guess you will too then!

Do you like your bedroom? I spent a weekend pulling your room apart. I bought a big new cube book shelf and turned your room into a study. It appears that at different times we all spend moments of time in your room. Liam and Chris giggled over your school yearbooks the other day!

The build up of the 12 month thing is starting to tell now. The family has decided to keep close on Easter Monday and also the 9th

April when I have arranged to have the day off work. Not sure what we'll do yet, but everyone is finding it a bit tricky to concentrate. We shall, as always, plough on. There is still laughter and music in the home which is always inclusive of you Kieran. Always. You will be forever a part of us. It has been quite lonely in a sense over the last few weeks. I experienced some self pity due to the fact that hardly anybody has enquired after us for months. People find it hard to step into our shoes, particularly parents whom want to be caring for us. They all cry if we discuss the loss of a child. People hurt imagining the grief, so they tend to stay away from us. For the same reason, I stay away from mums.

However, I can now say that I'm a grizzly whinger, because I've had four mums reach out this last week to say that they are thinking of us with Easter coming up. We give the impression that we cope well and don't need anyone. And we do cope well. Keeping busy makes the days blur and keeps the pain in its place for a time. Anyway, you are here with us often Kieran and sharing both the good and bad.

Please though, help us get through the next couple of weeks in a way that would make you proud of us Kieran.

We miss you so deeply.

I love you. Mum

17th March, 2008
Hey babe!
Yesterday, Mal and I were in Torquay for the Otway Classic road bike event. We went to the foreshore markets . . . and so did you! It seems that whenever you flit by, my Reiki hands get hot and prickle. So there we were, wandering from stall to stall when my hands began to burn. I told Mal that you were with us, which was nice.

I spotted a stall that had sage sticks and buzzed over there for a look. I asked for sage and Lisa, the stall holder and I began to talk about my need for sage and the ballet shop. Lisa then told me quote, "I'm being told you need to put a mirror in the doorway and other things with sea salt and jade plants." Hmm. I asked her if she did readings. Aahh . . . A Reiki master whom does readings. Cool! Somehow we got around to our "losing" you Kieran and whaddya know . . . Lisa began to give me messages to me, from you. You sent me messages that were things I had been confused about. You felt that I had been busy teaching you the things you needed to know to get to 17, and no, I hadn't hurt you and you felt I was a good mum . . . and you thanked me for the things I did for you. (You are very welcome by the way. I just wish our road together had been less complicated.)

I had been confused about whether I could call you or not, maybe you were busy? No, I can call you anytime, for anything. You can do more to help me from where you are now than if you had stayed here. You feel sad when I'm sad and you don't like me to be like that. Things will be better and I will have more children in my life to help. I will be a "wonderful grandmother." You haven't missed anything and been a part of all family events. You don't feel that you have missed out on anything.

Apparently you and I used to "muck around" between lives and although it is not time for me to go yet, we will muck around again. Yep, you'll be there when I get there! Now, that issue was one causing me anxiety – I don't want you going anywhere before I get there! You will appear to me as I need you to, i.e.: Kieran form.

So then, Lisa had managed to answer all these things I worried about with your help. Thank you so much! Firstly, your visit did a lot for me. It confirmed to me that when my hands "go off", you are indeed visiting. Secondly, you were aware how much I have been dreading Easter and you shared a great deal of love with me. I felt and still feel so reassured by your presence that the "loss" part seems more bearable. Thirdly, I learnt more about the spirit – human body connection. It was so lovely to know you were right there answering my questions. I couldn't get enough! Poor Lisa . . . she had a stall to run yet there she was, hugging me!

I'll add in things as I recall them – here is another. I am to look out for feathers as this is how you'll identify yourself. Sure enough, to test my concentration, there on a billboard on the way home was a giant feather! See, I'm paying attention.

Oh, and an event happened on Saturday in Torquay that reminded me of how human and frail I can be . . .

I was waiting at the finish line with all the "other wives" for the Otway Classic riders to come in. The riders were being diverted to a section of safe road, before entering the finish area. Whilst I sat on a pylon, casually watching all the movement I was jolted into shock by a huge "bang". An older, bearded rider had been hit by a car doing a U-turn in front of him and slamming his head into the door. Everything and everyone went still and into shock. Including me! The rider managed to regain his feet and stood with his bike between his legs, looking stunned staring into the car. The driver didn't move. No-one moved. The damn flies stopped buzzing! I found myself getting to my feet, thinking an Official must surely be rushing to help but beginning to realise that help wasn't forthcoming. I began to walk over. Then I ran when my nursey side checked in and this chap remained clearly in shock. Blood was pouring down his face. I grabbed his arm and spoke to him and he turned to me, looking like a stunned mullet. I asked him some questions and gradually watched him come into focus. He began to move and eventually thought he could ride on. The official up the road a bit, merely called out to him to, "come on mate, ride up to the first aid tent." So shakily, away he went. I wandered back to my spot, sitting next to a nice lady whom made disparaging remarks about the lad driving the car. To my horror, I began to cry and shake. I was deeply affected by the moment and also angry that no-one else helped this chap. I had to explain to my new friend that I had lost you Kieran (well kind of) and found this road business unsettling. It took me ages to settle down. I felt quite disturbed. Obviously my core is still fragile. I know I'm much jumpier and couldn't begin to imagine ever going back to E.R. or trauma rooms for a career.

I did wonder though, what this event meant as a part of a spiritual thing. Was I being tested for something on the week of my son's anniversary of death? Or did the world stop, specifically for me to get up and check the biker dude? For what purpose? Did I pass or fail? Or was it all a coincidence? No, there are no such things as coincidence. Life is a series of events and learning situations.

So Kieran, I found that event very traumatic but I can't help but wonder whom the event was meant for . . .

Your bewildered mother!

19th March, 2008
Morning Kieran,
You are my first thought of every day – which means basically that I wake up and my stomach lurches! I will never forget though, the deep, deep agony of early mornings of last year. Every morning was shock, denial, more shock, and agony. I hated to wake up. Now, I still hate to wake up, still feel sick, but there is some level of acceptance, which allows me to still get up each day.

Two more days and horror of horrors, Good Friday appears. I am quite confused by the event. Firstly, Easter has appeared early so by lunar events this is your anniversary time but then by dates we have to go through it all again in two weeks. Secondly, this is also a time of remembering Jesus.

I was inclined to bypass this entire thing until Liam, Bless him, mentioned that he is going to get Bid and Chris something because he doesn't want the kids to think of Easter as a terrible thing. Good thought Scoobs! So, I shall be led by the young folk in our home. I even picked up hot cross buns yesterday! I also put a memoriam in the paper for both days (Easter Monday and 9th of April) which was the only thing I could think of to help me decide which day was the priority Anniversary day. You died at Easter which is an important event. Yet you also have a date of death . . . so which do we remember? Obviously both since Easter works on a lunar count! So then don't forget to check the Herald Sun lad! I phoned your dad too and had a nice chat.

I have 9th April off and your dad thinks he may have lunch with us that day. So now, here is what I wanted to discuss with you Kieran . . .

Yesterday, I took Karen to Pioneer Park in Berwick, to the school house for lunch. We sat outside and began our relaxation. Wouldn't you know it . . . a police car arrived, driving across the park. Then another, followed by an ambulance, then another ambulance! No sirens. They used the vehicles to block our view and someone around us from inside said that they had found a body under the pergola in the park middle. Karen and I just looked at each other. Then, the Alfred Rescue helicopter appeared and parked beside us! It was huge and immensely noisy, dust flew everywhere. My gut lurched hugely . . . Karen asked me if I wanted to leave and I seriously considered it! Then I decided to "get over it." However, after some consulting and fussing around, and presumably doing something useful with a person or a body, the helicopter began to prepare for take-off. The door which was open and exposing bedding and equipment was slammed shut. The rotor blades began to race and the whirring got louder and louder. We were unable to hear, see or feel anything, but the presence of this chopper.

My gut clenched, nausea rose to the back of my throat as a ball of bile and I could no longer eat. It was a brave effort by Alexandra that crumbled. I could see my lovely baby on the stretcher, drips and frantic staff pumping the air-viva desperately fighting for your life while the copter warmed up, hurrying desperately to get you to the Alfred. I saw it; I heard it, felt it. The tears welled up and the grief arrived. My baby going through terrible things – I *know* what you went through. I was an E.R. nurse. . . . awful, horrid. Karen tossed over her serviette, eyes full of tears. Away went the Alfred helicopter. Survival of another . . . what . . . ? Message . . . ? Event . . . ? Trick . . . ? Joke . . . ? Learning experience?

What are the chances of that Alfred helicopter (your rescue team) turning up at my lunch table on my only day off in months, in Berwick on the week of the anniversary of my son's death? Hmm.

Karen was stunned. Shaking her head at the "coincidences", we moved back to the car. As we walked, I noted two magpie feathers and picked them up, smiling . . .

29th March, 2008

I woke up today on holidays Kieran! We are in Pacific Palms resort, 40kms south of Taree! Chris and Bridget have been accompanied by a close friend each to our three bedroom unit alongside the beach. Liam stayed at home and is having friends over for a barbeque tea tonight. He will be off to Europe in two months with Nick, so he thought he better stay home and earn some spending money.

We flew to Newcastle last night (where I went to school!) then picked up a hire Tarago and drove up north. The four kids are down at the beach and we're hanging around . . . exhausted!

We have arrived through the trauma of Easter 2008, something I'd been dreading. Good Friday duly arrived on 21st March, 2008 with a full moon – a non-spectacular full moon that is. I had already been in tears all day before due tension build up.

Chris is not doing well in school and is in danger of continuing this way. I am fatigued and miserable at work, and I'm thinking of leaving. Other issues arise . . . and so on and on . . . and on. I've been setting my survival goals by units of events. i.e.: end of term, then Easter, then a friend's wedding, then holidays, etc.

On Easter Friday the family had a special breakfast with hot cross buns (which I never imagined eating again in my life . . . but they *are* in memory of Jesus). We dedicated a prayer to Jesus and Kieran. The guys all had wanted to go off and visit friends and attend functions, which they did . . . but yet still came home often and for long periods of time. In fact we enjoyed for the most part, a quiet and family orientated time. Mal and I went to an Easter Sunday wedding for friends which was lovely but, again, I had been dreading. I didn't do so well at the last wedding Kieran! It tears at me that I will never see you married, or having babies. However, I largely managed to stay to the end and that was probably due to the fact that I spent hours cuddling little Zac, another of our lovely friends' baby.

Easter Monday arrived with bad weather. Over the long weekend I had flashbacks of last Easter – moments of memories, gut wrenching, painful memories and moments re-lived. I woke Good Friday early am and couldn't sleep, imagining the details of your entrapment and journey thereafter. It seems horrific and induced tears on and off over the four days. However, with it came the resignation. Acceptance I suppose. I can't turn back time. I can't change events. I can't bring you back. I can't stand you in front of me and hold you and tell you I wish I had done such and such . . .

I wish I could.

So, Easter passed.

Hmm, my hands are heavily prickling as I write this – I know you are here. I was so stressed up to now – I scared myself with the amount of anxiety and stress I've carried. My gut is clenched, along with fists, shoulders and chest – something worrying has been happening in my head too. I feel that my soul has split in half. I've been so distressed that I've divided into the half person whom must continue function and show civility and then the other half becomes the person with no hope, no energy, and no joy. I have on one hand, the opportunities to grow and develop in many directions – teaching, nursing, buying into retail, natural therapies, travel and so on. And the ideas grab me . . . briefly. Then the other side prevents. I am sluggish, heavy, uninterested, unopportunistic, grief-filled and unable to perform. I grow weary of nursing, tired of growing, fatigued with coping. Maybe this week of holidays will help.

Love Mum

Wednesday, 2nd April, 2008

Today is our wedding anniversary, which began with a boat trip out to sea, to see the dolphins. We enjoyed lunch out on the pier and then, while the guys went swimming, I went to a natural healing centre. I had a detoxification via foot spa, Bowen's therapy, Myofacial release and then Reiki – all for $50. My healing practitioner began to educate me in these methods, even offering me well priced equipment if I wish and all the paperwork I would like to take with me. I was a little sceptical until the Reiki because I could feel the connection and see the colours. Why did he treat me as a colleague more than a patient? He told me that he could detect I have a "good connection" and he was very glad to have met me. This was different but nice.

However, these details do add to my thoughts list – perhaps a natural healing centre of my own. I am beginning to plan ahead a little and visualise a future.

Reiki, Bowens, foot spa and maybe kinesiology?

This week has been a lovely one, with rest at times. At the same time, we have done some fun things too. The four guys are due for their third surf lesson tomorrow and watching them from our beach towels is hardly stressful! The week is going so fast though . . . I find myself day dreaming heaps too. I am not very grounded *and* I love being off with the Spirits, so tend to be half here.

I have been reflecting to myself on my journey this year, as in since you changed form Kieran. What have I learnt? Firstly, these are my conclusions post research and gathered from my own experiences, several different churches and their philosophies, endless reading, endless prayer, study and some bizarre events. Since starting off as a little Methodist girl and following my journey, it has become clear to me that there is a Great Creator. This God is the same God that everybody prays to whether he is called God, Great Creator, Allah, Jehovah, Wakan Tanka, the Trinity or anything else. No religion is more important than any other. How can it be? We all love the same God and God is love. So then, to make God happy we need to love each other as well as Him. That means dropping all judgements and becoming respectful and tolerant of each other's differences.

To disperse His love, God has allowed Major Prophets to become obvious in all cultures. Therefore, Mohammad, Jesus, Buddha and other major figureheads have all had a major role in spreading the word of God, which is *love*.

Our purpose in being here is to learn how to love and forgive, through all varieties of experiences. We have chosen our families and friends and major events before we arrive in human form. Then our life is about learning and growing before returning again to the spirit world.

So Kieran, you have returned to our loving home with the Great Creator. Then, in its shortest version, back we go again in our next lives to learn something different. So that is Version Alex!

And personally? Let's see, I still have not learnt patience despite our best efforts Kieran. Whenever I was stressed and yelling, you would wrap your arm around my shoulder and say "slow down mum, it's all okay." Actually, you were always quite calming and even succeeded in making me feel silly!

I am also prone to making judgemental remarks like when stuck behind drivers that do silly things or seem to drive too slowly. "You stupid old bat!" I'll say. I'm also too cheeky for anyone's good sometimes.

Oh yeah! I have heaps to learn. And these days, as a grieving mum? Well now . . . My biggest challenge is to renew caring about events outside my home again. I do not have energy any more to nurse or be a good friend, or be a good mum or wife. Maybe soon, I can learn the secret steps to giving when you feel "gived out" and all burnt up.

6th April, 2008

One year today since your accident. I couldn't sleep all night and finally crawled into bed after 3am. I could feel your presence all around me. The house moved with strange sounds and I inexplicably knew you were wandering around checking on everyone. I sat for a while remembering the events of your accident and each moment thereafter.

I still couldn't sleep until way after 4am. Then my mobile phone rang at 5am, but it came up with anonymous on it. At 6am the door bell rang and Bridget appeared at the front door after being returned to us by an irate parent where she had been sleeping over. Bid and her two mates had snuck off overnight and the police spent the night looking for them. We sent her to bed, too angry to make sense of the events. It was then I noticed the glass water feature ball was running. It was off at 3am and I knew you were restless. After asking everyone in the house, nobody had turned the ball on. So, can I suppose that you were worrying about your sister, Kieran?

7th April, 2008

Kieran, I wanted to tell you about my strange Saturday at the cemetery. I met your friend Locky, Kieran. You mentioned him to me a few times and he had made an impression on you. I can see why. I am uncertain why he felt it so important to meet with me, but he did. I warmed to him immediately. You already know that you have a party organised for Wednesday, 9th April, 2008, to remember you and our combined journeys over the 12 months. I really do think that it is cheating to know about surprise parties just because you live in the Spirit World!

Anyway, Locky seems delighted to receive an invitation. I hope it will be a lovely night. If you have any pull in "Heaven", do you think you could organise some lovely weather with some stars for Wednesday night??

Mum xxxx

9th April, 2008
One year today since you moved out.

2am – 10th April, 2008 – Events

We all stayed home from work and school except poor ole Mal, whom dragged his tired body off to work. We did the rounds of the florist, the grog shop, party shop, grocery shop, cemetery to say hi to you . . .
Martin phoned and cancelled lunch, so we instead met with your Rumanian brother Nick, at the kebab shop where Cam looked after us. Mick woke me with a beautiful message on my phone, wishing us all smiles and love today. He was talking to you at the cemetery before work, 7.30am. Lovely lad he is. Then I opened the front door in preparation for collecting the morning paper, and smacked straight into a huge flower arrangement from TFM, your old work mates.

I had a quick read of the paper and located our memorial message to you, before SMS messages flew in from Pop and Shirley.

Man, you sure draw some attention!

Denise came over to help prepare at 3pm. Mick, your buddy came over at 5pm for an hour on his way to Daniel and Tash's.

Then 7pm, the floodgates broke and people poured in! Considering 7.30pm was kick off time, people were eager! The first two hours

I went from person to person meeting and greeting. There was laughter and hugs, drinking and eating. Kieran, the feeling was so nice! The atmosphere was loving and great. So many people came up and gave me hugs, even every boy!

You had buddies from each part of your life, school and work. They all remembered and came to reminisce. I put yellow and blue flowers out to make the occasion bright. You were with us because I felt your presence. Several people commented on your presence! People told me they felt you, or their necks prickled, or you were seen . . . Locky said you were "everywhere man – here, there, here, there." Nicole said "you were there alright . . . you were everywhere!" so I guess you were excited to have such a party. Great wasn't it?!

Locky has a clear connection to the spiritual world which is interesting because I know how drawn you were to him. He later told me that while he was driving to our house for your party, you kept telling Locky to "drive faster" and "Hurry Up"! Some things don't change Kieran do they!

Locky played his guitar, sorry, Liam's guitar and kept background music going. Then Dan, from Kambrya played the song he wrote for you. People cried. Dan has since recorded this song. I think it's called, "Only the Good Die Young." We had a little speech, giving thanks for our blessings, each other and you, whom we miss desperately. Then, we charged our glasses to you. It was an amazing evening because it was all about you. But it was also a mix of ages and interests. We all invited anyone we thought relevant and tossed it all around – anyone who loved you was the criteria, whilst keeping it small. I actually thought we'd have 20-30 people, but I should have realised!

The only damp spot was that your dad sent a message saying he wasn't up to a visit. A real shame because everyone in our household the next day expressed a real sense of peace and contentment. We actually felt that we had partied with you and we all had a really caring and fun time.

So that's how we coped with the first anniversary of you passing.

A lady in the USA called Dr Meg Blackburn-Losey has written about the Indigo Children and the "Children of Now" who are young and aware people – the new generation of children and young people that bring knowledge of "Heaven" directly with them to try and prepare the world for the way of the Great Creator. They bring messages.

Kieran, I believe you were amongst the first of this new generation and your role of being so aware of spiritual things (although you were hardly perfect in terms of behaviour) and leaving behind messages for so many people was synchronised to lead the way for the Indigo Children. I wrote an email to Dr Meg expressing this and within 12 hours, she had written back words of encouragement and support to a grieving mother. I felt so touched to hear back from her.

27th April, 2008
New Age Fair – Siobhan, Bridget and I tootled along to the New Age Expo in Berwick and spent several hours there having a ball. Within minutes, I was standing at a stall trying out all the Tibetan singing bowls and allowing a bowl to choose me! Which it did! I love it and am told that it will increase the vibrations in our household and help clear out negativity. To my surprise, Bid began to take an interest. We looked at everything – Reiki massages, had aura photos taken, bought crystals – it was great. Both girls had readings done which were caring and supportive, positive messages. Bridget, I think, will need to hear from you soon Kieran. A few times she has made a comment about you not turning up for her. I know different

of course because you do visit her at night, but she will need to find this out for herself.

I picked up brochures about courses I think I should do also. At the crystal stall, after I asked a question about crystals, the vendor asked to place a hand on my shoulder. Puzzled and a smidge wary, I agreed. He stood there with his eyes closed for a moment, then turned me to face him. He looked at me and announced, "Your son is telling me that he misses hugging you. He wants me to give you a hug from him." "Oh" I replied with huge surprise and found myself enveloped in a massive and long hug. This comment had triggered a memory of my last reading from Rene which included your statement of how much you miss our hugs. Thank you Kieran for your hug. Hope you got a hug out of it too. I was a little surprised to say the least, but all too soon it was over! Wow, I am so lucky to have this connection to you.

While I think of it, I had a visit I think from my Grandad Nelson, whom I remember from when I was five. He appeared at my last reading. When I was at work last week, then in and out of my car, I kept smelling really strong cigarette, almost cigar smoke. I just couldn't find the source anywhere. I asked everyone around me and I checked my car. My car has never been smoked in! Finally, I was forced to concede that maybe, I had a visitor! I thought about Grandad as the only spirit I may know of that smoked strong cigs, only I wasn't sure if he smoked at all. I phoned dad in New Zealand, "Dad, did your father smoke at all?" "Yes he did" replied dad, "quite strong cigarettes they were. Why do you ask?" I answered, "I think your dad has been visiting me and watching what I'm getting up to!" "Well that's nice of him" noted my dad.

Sometimes, when I float around on this lovely spiritual plane and I can sense and feel Spirits around me, I manage to put things in wafty perspective. The pain is less and I understand a bit of the *big picture*. Other times, when I'm being a human and travelling my journey, the pain is unbearable. I jolt to earth and remember that my poor little family is torn and battered and they all need so much love and support. I remember that my baby has really died in a tragic car accident and my ovaries and uterus ache with a mother's pain. The hole in my chest hasn't healed and I will never feel whole and complete again.

It would be so much easier to float around in hippy land and become permanently wafty! But heck, wafty time will have to wait because this life demands that I teach my children survival, love, forgiveness, respect and whatever they need to go through the modern world.

It's a pretty big swing from one reality to another Kieran. I have also become aware that you are now no longer 17, but rather ancient by earth years. I understand that you visit me in teenage form. I appreciate this because I like being your mum and I don't want this taken away from me.

1st May, 2008
Hey Kieran!
I thought of Mick, your best buddy just now and began to text him a hello. I felt strongly that you would want me to send a message to him from you. I heard "G'day" so I wrote this in my SMS. Then heard "add mate", so I wrote, 'G'day mate' and indicated that this was a message to Mick from you. I worried that he would think me nutty so I questioned it. I knew you were beside me, because I saw watery movement beside me, and my "Reiki" hands were burning. I "heard" in my head somewhere – "send it." I asked back, "Are you sure?" again, the words, "send it" came into my head. I asked myself if I was having a conversation with myself when an impatient, "*Just send it*" crashed into my head. I sent it.

Two minutes later, I received a phone call from Mick! He told me that he was with Daniel and the boys. They had just finished putting R.M. Williams bull horns on Daniel's new HQ Holden ute, as well as a Bundy sticker. At the exact moment, our message arrived; your ute song came on their music machine. You were having a drink with the boys they told me and your message sent by me unknowingly, confirmed your presence to them. Cool! They were rapt! Daniel says the ute is Daniel and Kieran's ute! Although it is quote, "A bloody woeful ute! It needs heaps of work!" Better than the bus I told them!

10th May, 2008
The last few days I've been shaky and over-anxious without seemingly knowing why. I pinned a reason unexpectedly today – its Mother's Day tomorrow. I took you some flowers and tidied up at the cemetery but came to tears when I placed my koru, New Zealand earring on your rose plant over your grave. It signifies the fact that the paua shell is kiwi, the earring is from me to you and the koru or spiral is about everlasting or continuous life. That core bit of me that I cover up leaked out and our familiar grief bit in deep.

Then a phone call from Mick revealed that Daniel's court case is scheduled for 26th May. I feel sick.

11th May, 2008
Mother's Day. Liam, Chris and Bid spoilt me with hugs and gifts of course. I also took a drive to Yarragon with Mal to meet Mandy and the boys. While waiting for them, Mal and I visited the local store which sold old fashioned sweets. I wasn't surprised Kieran, when you dropped in sending me our song. I felt my hands burn and leaned in towards Malcolm to whisper "Kieran's here", at exactly the same time that Mal flipped out a poster of a skater which seemed just like you. Thank you for your visit. I know you were checking on me. For the most part, I'm okay but man, I sure miss you.

I had a few phone messages from folk with you in mind – your dad Martin, Siobhan, Shirley, Karen and Lisa.

I also stopped in at the cemetery on the way home – beautifully full of Mother's Day flowers. Lots of mums buried in there. So filled with love, our Berwick cemetery.

I love you. Mama

17th May, 2008

Thirteen months. Still I count each month. I've cried a lot this month. I can't seem to remember things. I keep parking the car badly. I have headaches and have difficulty fitting my life into my life! I wonder sometimes if everything has finally taken its toll. Maybe I'm brain damaged!

I know heaps of things are going on. I'm trying to buy mum a car and run around to car yards and banks. I have also found a New Age shop that Bill and I could buy into together. I have an appointment with a financial advisor about these figures. I *still* await the dance shop figures. This idea of being a partner in the dance shop is very obviously not going to occur. I just wish that the lady concerned would simply say so but again I shall have to be the one to state the obvious. This is the sort of thing that tires me. With honest communication I would have let go of this idea long ago. I hate being played with. Meanwhile Bid needs transport every day to dance classes for various commitments – sometimes twice a day after school (and I already pick up and drop off two kids at two different schools as there is no bus).

Today Bid had her dance audition for her scholarship at school. Although we haven't made a big deal out of it, she is still exhausted and so am I. I hope that this all pays off for her because Bid is such a hard worker.

Work is exhausting at nine hours a day – no lunch or coffee breaks. We always try, but somehow we are always so busy that we are shocked when the day ends and we haven't eaten!

Ultimately though, this week's internal turmoil involves the court case. I finally found a minute to call Senior Detective Denise whom told me that although the proceedings have been instigated, Daniel will have a couple of Committal Hearings for an Adjournment, twice, then finally, we'll get our Committal Hearing at Melbourne Magistrate's Court . . . eventually . . . maybe up to two years away. My heart went into overdrive initially, but now, I'm quite deflated because I don't see closure for a long time.

Daniel meantime, is married and will probably have kids by then. I don't want the guys to get an extreme punishment and certainly don't wish to see Daniel in jail but he is being tried for dangerous driving causing death and that will have a consequence of something nasty.

As for us, we try to patch our lives as much as possible. That old adage of, "life goes on" is true and stinks, but one has to keep going. There has been a huge amount of pain in our family, but my guys are a tough bunch and they get up again after each punch. We do it as a team. With love.

It is important that we pull together when there has been so much for the family to deal with. Not only have you children had to adjust to being in divorced family situations with ongoing issues, but each of us experienced other painful life events. For Liam it was the death of his best friend Nick's dad and then their basketball coach all in the same six months as losing you. For Aimee and Chris, their losses involved the death of their stepfather by suicide, their grandmother and you all in the same year. We all struggled at losing my brother-in-law David to cancer a year before you went. Most parents help their families learn that death is normal. I have found myself thinking that I need to teach my children that it is normal to live. When you add in other significant losses to this family, the number is large. How do I explain that death is a normal event? They have lost a fundamental belief that life can be good. I want them to trust that they can go forward and experience a happy future but their childhood experiences suggest otherwise. Mal and I have our work cut out for us.

Anne at work told me about your conversation with her – you know about our family and how we are close and get through things together, and how much you love your mum. Oh baby! Hearing this from Anne is such a nice thing to hear. Knowing how close you and I are Kieran, makes this a little easier in some ways, but also makes it unbearable because I want my boy here (in the flesh I mean).

I played your school friend Dan's song *"Only the Good Die Young"* that he wrote for you. It is great but naturally, I cried. I cry a lot compared to the old me. Mostly, our hearts still feel tattered. Thank God I still have the three kids and Mal. I couldn't imagine losing an entire family like those in the Burma Hurricane or the China Earthquake, or a war. It is awful that so many people struggle.

Mal is flying to Noumea tomorrow for a working week in a mine compound. He isn't looking forward to it, but hopefully it will be a positive experience. Please keep an eye on him son.

I love you, mum xxxx

24th May, 2008

I'm aware of having slipped into a new phase of grief. I saw our 14 month moon this week Kieran. It was huge and ringed with layers of yellow haze, brightly beaconing. Bridget commented that it looked sad to her. I agree. It reflected my heart exactly. I have noticed that I'm bubbling around, not thinking of the Kieran little things as much and initially thinking to myself that I'm healing, oh my gosh! Then to my horror, I began to understand that underneath it all . . . the Grief Monster lurks!

The Grief Monster sits quietly in the pit of my being. Whenever a little Kieran moment flicks into my consciousness, the Grief Monster stirs. I quickly shake off the thought and I am safe for a while. Sometimes, the Grief Monster takes a little stroll towards the light and I begin to panic. Tears well, I begin to swear frequently. I shake my head and begin my well developed habit of pushing the Grief Monster back into its cavern. That ball of grief has grown into a being, an unruly and unpredictable life of huge proportions. The Grief Monster fights me several times a day and gives me nightmares at sleep time. Whereas before I freely revelled in being Kieran obsessed, now I have settled into the opposite. I wondered why I was coping so well Kieran. It appears that I have given birth to this appendage. All Hail the Grief Monster!

Every so often, if I haven't felt a deep grief episode for a little while (as in a day or two), I worry that I'm leaving my Kieran behind and I poke the edges of the Grief Monster merely by thinking of you and sweeping my memory bank. Well, I'm both relieved and mortified to feel that ole Monster jump right on up with lumbering speed and clutch at the back of my throat. Man, that monster has speed!

So, what happens long term when you push down your monsters so that you can function in the real world? Is it damaging? I wonder as I am very obviously, to me at any rate, split into two beings. This journey of losing a child is about losing myself. Does that sound absurd? Man, I am so tired. So weary. Coping, coping . . .

Every day I deal with new people. Lots of new people and many of them with sad stories. Most of them ask questions of their nurses. Do you have children? How many children do you have? Are they boys or girls? Oh, I have five . . . no four . . . um, I mean three. Aah, I have three living with me, one whom is living away and soon to have a baby and ah . . . one who is floating around somewhere . . .

Sometimes it is easier that people flow in and out never knowing my agonies. But since I'm at work 10 hours a day and we are a small team which is way too busy to ever give me a thought, sometimes I feel so lonely in my grief.

The truth is Kieran that I think of you constantly, a zillion thoughts a day. I'm very careful to keep my thoughts fleeting and never focus in case the Grief Monster leaps out, but the spot between the Monster and I is small and tight. No matter how much I laugh and joke, which is pretty much all day, it is war underneath. Sometimes I win, then I panic in case I've pushed you away and prod the Monster, then I groan and battle it down!

I stopped to cry after writing all that. The Grief Monster has its moment and won the episode. I have terrible flashbacks of your battered and swollen body, and the tears trickling down your cheeks whilst you were in a coma.

This journey of grief is a lonely and miserable road to travel.
Mum xoxo

4th June, 2008

I had a dream last night. You and I were on a sports field Kieran. You sat in a wheelchair with your right leg stretched out in a leg brace. You and the people around you were in grey school type sports uniform. I was pushing you across the field. Young people wandered around us.

You turned your head towards me and said, "I need a piss mum" and I turned the chair towards the toilet blocks. I wheeled you into the toilet block and into the first cubicle on the right. There was no door. You pushed off the wheelchair arms with both hands and stepped onto your legs. But your right braced leg wouldn't hold you up and you stumbled onto your left leg to weight bear. I automatically leant in behind you with my left leg forward. My front was pressed into your back, taking some of your weight. I'm shorter, so I leaned my head into your neck. I know your body well. I'm your mum. I have rubbed your back, dressed your wounds, cut your hair many, many times. I smelt your hair and you grabbed my left thigh to steady yourself. I looked around while you toileted and you kept your hand on my leg. I could feel your body, the warmth of your hand, the warmth and smell of your body familiar to me. It felt right that I was with you as your mum, your friend, your support. A pang of sadness flashed through me at your disability, but I didn't want to be anywhere else.

Without warning, I snapped awake, shocked. Where did my son go? I remembered, and the familiar Grief Monster began to surface. I couldn't move. The warmth and heavy imprint of your hand remained on my leg for long afterwards. Long minutes passed and the tears began to roll down my cheeks as I again began to process my loss. It took a while, but I later started to think. Your visit seemed so real.

I felt you, saw you, heard you and smelt you Kieran even long after I woke. I theorised that I've become a little distant from you Kieran and I guess I have been both protecting my never healing heart and also trying not to be a pest to you Kieran.

I think Kieran that you are telling me that you are okay and you are still around us. Whether you had lived and needed care, or passed over to a free state, perhaps you still want your mum/buddy/companion. That's great by me because I need you Kieran. I will always love you and need you. Thank you for the connection. Funny, it's nearly 24 hours later and I can still feel the hand print!

Mum

13th June, 2008

Happy Birthday love of my life! 19 today! I hope you have a great day! Us? Well, tears all day and night yesterday. No doubt about it, it's raw and painful. For me, my misery of having the flu for two weeks just mixed around with my missing you. I'm plain miserable. But not for one second do I regret giving birth to you Kieran. Not one. I'm so honoured to have given birth to you and to have been the person to watch over and care for you. My heart may be broken but I still smile and laugh at your antics and the many memories of your love and indulgence towards a strict mother!

It is pouring and they call today Black Friday. That suits my heart state anyway. I shall go down to the cemetery today and place beautiful pink roses straight from my heart to you.

I love you.

Happy birthday! Mum

2nd July, 2008

Mal is home from Noumea and tells of great adventures! He was working in the nickel mines and not enjoying it at all! To top it off, he managed to get arrested by the French Police through language insufficiency! He is pleased to be home and I have been trying not to laugh at his highly indignant episodes of semi-trauma! They are amusing stories that he tells us but in reality, these incidents have stressed Mal a lot.

Liam left for Europe a week and a half ago. Emotionally, on the surface at least, I felt and feel okay about this. However, since he left I have lost a dozen things including my car and house keys which I still haven't found. My stress levels have shot up and I feel physically ill. I know I have been having ectopic/palpitations which were also detected by the doctor when I did my work physical. I passed as fit to work but need to have a halter monitor done. Nothing is wrong. It's just that I'm deeply off balance and struggling. I hear from your brother every few days so I know he is fine, but still . . .

Last week, we received a letter from Aimee wanting to make some amends. Her baby is due in seven weeks and I'm guessing that she is lonely. None of us know quite what to do with it all. Although the family remain deeply angry with Aimee (in fact we very rarely mention her), every so often I find myself thinking that I should try and find a reason for her behaviour. It is so difficult however due to the undeniable memories of her ongoing nonsense. Aimee's arrival into our home several years ago heralded a change towards stress and exasperation amongst us all.

Your sister, an angry Gothic wearing black and decorated with forearm slash marks, moved in with all the good grace of a pit-bull terrier. She was more interested in sleuthing out everyone's secrets and sneaking into her family's private life than making friends. I know you had more than one angry fight with her and you were not the only one. She was demanding, dishonest and self-righteous. All of you guys struggled with her. Many a time I could have easily suggested she move.

It is my belief that Aimee did not want to move in with us at all but she did not have anyone else to go to, having used up her welcome everywhere else.

I am trying to remember that Aimee's life had a lot going against her from the start. There has been so much ugliness and nastiness on Aimee's maternal side for such a lot of years that after a while you stop hoping that you can help.

Once someone digs themselves a hole and then they sit in it, you cannot dig them out unless they want to be dug out. Aimee is comfortable with drama. So comfortable that we have forgotten that it was Aimee at only 15 years old who found her Stepfather's body in the garage after a particularly gruesome suicide. The hours of counselling I took her to were useless because she would rather enjoy her dramas. She did not want our help then and she has not wanted it since. Until now.

I do not think I am willing to take on Project Aimee. I do not think I can even afford to think about her at all.

No surprise to anyone, I feel a guilt coming on however . . . worse than any headache. I have been this girl's stepmother since she was three.

Kieran, what should I do?

I can't allow our family anymore hurt. Chris has also lost his stepfather and yet he is respectful and loving to us, the family he has lived with since he was 12.

An enormous part of my rage toward Aimee is about you, of course. Not only did Aimee disrespect us while you were fighting for your life but she also reminds me that I failed you by trying so hard to help her!

On the day Aimee moved in, you were terribly ill. I spent the day helping Aimee to unpack and couldn't help noting that she was nervous, and needing attention. Aware that you were in pain, I checked in on you. You were so ill that I should have called an ambulance. You were seeped in a deep pool of sweat and dehydrated with a massive headache. I knew you had been trying light drugs. I washed you and changed your sheets, worrying but not acting on my usual instincts. It was not until much later that I understood you were coming off something.

With my mind running around in circles and me barely remembering to drop off and pick up the other two kids, I missed my nursing cues. Later on you confessed to me that you had been on "Ice". It seems to me that from that first day, I leant towards Aimee's more dramatic sense of getting help than leaning towards your quiet struggles with life.

Despite the fact that I took you both to counsellors and tried so hard to spend quality time with you, Aimee always kept me on my toes.

With my long hours at work and running a house with five teenagers, my moments with you were deep and real but too few. You began to spend more time away from home. Of course you always were running about seeking new adventures but now even more so.

I took my eyes off you to watch Aimee. When I lost you, it was a very great challenge for me not to blame Aimee. I will leave this for a moment as it makes me dizzy.

There has also been a big upset with Mal's mum and I am not much interested in spending any energy sorting this one out. I am fatigued.

However, I have felt you around me often recently and I am at peace to know that you are here with me.

Kieran, I feel that you have been trying to tell me something. I asked God if something could be teed up to allow a Medium to guide me. I thought I could also ask about my job direction and Aimee's intent. I phoned a different Medium yesterday and have an appointment today! I wonder if you will visit me today Kieran. I love messages from you . . .

Later . . . Wow, I sure learnt heaps today. I was encouraged to keep studying. I was given positive news about each of your brothers and sisters. Aimee was given the rather sluggish half tick of approval and I was advised to do nothing about my work situation just now. I would know sometime soon when its time. So I shall do nothing! Then lovely lad, at last . . . you sent me a beautiful message that I cried through. The Medium translated for me word for word:

"I see you mum, I didn't want you to be hurt the way you are . . .
I see you . . . but I can do more on this side . . .
I love you . . . you know that . . . I always will.
You're so brave and so beautiful but so hard on yourself . . . please don't be.
You can't save everybody and change everything and everyone. They have their own paths to walk and lessons to learn. Just love them all and let them do it.
I am there with you all; all the times you need me to be.
I so love you.
Thank you for being my mum . . ."

Hesitate while I cry my eyes out . . .

"Mummy, don't cry . . . be happy because I am free now.

I will see you again when your turn comes. No more heartache mum, no more heartache.
Easier times ahead. Be happy. I love you.

And not for a long time will you lose another . . . not for a long time . . ."

And so I continued to cry – of course, since I never do what I am told! However Kieran, I listened to the tape several times and with writing down your message, I'll read it every day and feel soothed.

You have to know Kieran that I am hopelessly incomplete without you and that you are my soul mate.

I truly don't want to do this life journey without you.
Mum

5th July, 2008
Since I don't get the choice about the days that insist on rolling forward, it is now 5th July, 2008 . . . Let me tell you that the beautiful song Dan sang on your anniversary, called "*Only the Good Die Young*" was played with his group *Saving Grace* (which in other circumstances you may have been a part of) at last night's Battle of the Bands round One. They introduced your song and attached it in memory of Kieran Browne.

Dan, being a lovely lad, gave me a copy. It really is beautiful.

7pm. Today has been a beautiful and amazing Kieran day. I began by reading your message. Then I found old tapes from previous readings and listened to them. I heard again your message from 30th April, 2007, your passing over time. Then I found some tapes – one from when you were a little boy . . . a yellow tape with, "Kieran's songs" on it. Remember?

I found one full of your songs – ones you copied onto a tape. I turned it on so you could listen to them while I did odd jobs around the house, sometimes stopping to do a little dance with you. I could feel your presence and knew you were tuned in.

By late afternoon, I decided to phone Marie who is the lady I met at the Berwick Psychic Fair and will be teaching me psychic development. The course begins on Thursday, so I phoned to find out details. All of a sudden, Marie asked me out of the blue . . ."Who is Daniel?" "Why do you ask that?" I wanted to know.

She told me that my son was with her hopping from one foot to another then, jumping in and out of a wheelchair saying, "Now I'm in a wheelchair, now I'm not!"

Last time I spoke to Marie, she apparently had visits from you for days, hearing you saying, "Can I speak to mum?" Each time you visited her, you kept saying, "Give mum the name Daniel, she will understand . . . tell her Daniel."

So today I told her about both your Daniels – the driver and the singer. Then I told her about your "visit" to me in a wheelchair weeks ago. It all began to make sense to her!

Marie tells me that you are going to help me study because there is work for us to do. The young warriors returning to God are to help the people here learning about the spiritual things on Earth in preparation for the events to be . . . which I as yet have no idea about. I do understand that God has work for us all to do and it is important and that time is running out. I also learned that Liam, Bid and I are all very old souls with learning to do and Malcolm is with me to support my journey.

Kieran, you going across to God now accelerates my journey of learning as well as giving you important jobs to do known only by you. My Spirit Guide will also always be by my side. It all began to make sense. I must try and deal with my grief but also know that I have to keep going and learning.

Now, my Kieran day continued because Marie informed me that you are always around me (which obviously I know). This came to the fore not long after my call. I picked up Liam's itinerary to Europe and asked out loud where a particular hotel was located. Two minutes later, Marilyn sent an SMS telling me that Liam is in Rumania still, in a new hotel and visiting family! Well, that answered that question.

I felt that you and I have had such a lovely shared day. Oh, and I did have a big cry on the last song on your tape Kieran, then phoned Marie . . . so I'm pretty sure you dropped in on Marie hopping around just to make me laugh. It worked, because picturing you bouncing in and out of a wheelchair did in fact make me giggle. I have had a cuddly day Kieran, given that I long to hold you in my arms.

Mum xx

6th July, 2008

Even more Kieran visits! I am so lucky! Today we had visits from the Bowen's Practitioner and his wife that I met in Tuncurry. I bought a detox foot bath from him and we were lucky enough to have this delightful couple personally deliver it and stay for lunch. What lovely people. This lovely lady is very spiritually aware and was distracted by your visits. I knew you were around today but was taken by surprise when she announced over lunch that she was approached by you. She later told me that you were very "persistent"! That's the Kieran I know!

Today's message involved a warning to watch over Bridget, because you are worried about her. I wish I knew what I'm watching for though.

Love you, mama

14th July, 2008
Phew, what a heavy few days!

I started a psychic development class on Thursday night which I am a bit uncertain of and then Friday to Sunday night did Reiki again. This time I spent the course with three Reiki masters, one Reiki trainee master and six other lovely and spiritual people learning like me. Interestingly, all of them were quite advanced and connected to spiritual things. They were all beautiful, loving and positive people and they welcomed me warmly. I learnt heaps. I don't know why I felt I should repeat this class because I could easily have booked in for Reiki II, but I felt drawn to this particular group and I am very glad.

Of interest and yet also with some horror, was the development of a situation that I wish I could have avoided. During a session where I was receiving treatment, it came to my attention that my practitioner was struggling to stay with me. Finally, with a sob he apologised and removed himself. He had felt my deep grief and felt himself affected by it. This set off a chain reaction of my tears, his tears, down the line to the Master's tears. Oh blimey! I should have stayed home.

Somehow I always make my presence felt just like the proverbial drama queen. Just when I think I'm dealing with my grieving process then I find myself in a situation where it flicks right back at me . . . as though the Spirits say "Oh no . . . you haven't finished yet. Get crying!"
The way I see it, tears will choke me forever, so what's my rush!? Never mind, I passed my course and made new friends.

Kieran, your brother is in Germany and sick. He lost his crystal! He kept it with him as he promised me, then got sick. I was very concerned for him and his health but also understood that you were watching over him. I couldn't help but feel a little pleased when Liam messaged again to add a little sheepishly that he had lost his crystal and then got ill! It was nice that he acknowledged his crystal!

21st July, 2008
I have been thinking again Kieran! "Oh No," I hear you say! Well, as I look back over the years, it occurs to me that each life experience has been a stepping stone for other major events. It was at 15 years old that I was to experience my first loss by death. A friend from church was killed in a car accident by the drunk driver of an oncoming car. I began to ponder the ways of life after this and took note of how badly affected family and friends were.

I had wanted to be a nurse since I was little and thought of nothing else from the time I was seven and a patient in an Adelaide Hospital having had my tonsils removed. I was required to have an injection in my derriere and two nurses came into my room. Together they tipped me over and proceeded to jab me. However, the two nurses were busy catching up on gossip and were very giggly. In my ignorance and the shame of having my buttocks exposed, I was sure that they were laughing at me and my bottom! At that very moment, my life decision was made. I would become a nurse and I would *never* laugh at anyone's bum. *Never*!

The passionate dream of becoming a nurse became a reality and within only six weeks of passing my Preliminary Training, Death found me again. During my first week of being on the medical ward, I was given a very old and frightening woman to look after. She would dangle her scrawny arms and legs through the bars of the cot sides and beckon to me with her skinny finger. In a reedy and spooky voice, she would recite to me, her 17 year old nurse, "Come on love . . . come on love . . ." while peering at me over her long beaky nose. It made my hair stand on end!

Not long afterwards, to my horror, the woman passed away while I was giving her care and it was left to me to prepare her body for the morgue! The fear shot up a notch or two especially since it was night time, on a very old ward and in the middle of a thunder storm!

So Kieran, my journey towards experiencing loss went forth in regular leaps and bounds. There were patients I didn't know well and also patients I came to love, as well as occasional family members of previous patients and also children from long illness. When I became a midwife several years later, loss via death became a little harder. Stillbirths, brain damaged babies, tiny bundles of life too young to save kicking weenie legs and sucking thumbs until their little lives ebbed away . . . and finally the gradual loss of a baby girl at 10 days old due to Spina Bifida. This little one I "specialled" for days as carer to both babe and her parents.

Each loss I processed somewhere in my heart . . . each beautiful soul farewelled . . . and each experience then locked deep within me like a cavernous Pandora's Box.

Meantime Kieran, my own personal losses accumulated. The deaths of four grandparents added to two best friends, then two in-laws and finally, only a year before you Kieran, my brother-in-law David whom I was very fond of. Each loss had to be acknowledged, processed and grieved over. Each circumstance had its own issues. Stick a painful divorce in there and gosh, living is exhausting!

By the time we were faced with you leaving us Kieran, I no longer had any idea how to go about grief. I was and am a master of tucking away pain into some corner of my heart. There is a marvellous advantage to this. I can keep going against any adversity. I am my own hero! (Well, not really! Actually my hero is Nelson Mandela but that's another story . . .) Generally speaking, unless I let them, nobody need see me struggle. Handy! Downside? What to feel? What is important, what is not? When does one step down from survival mode? Does one step down from survival mode at all?

As far as losing a child goes, irreparable damage to one's heart is ensured. I already knew this before I experienced it for myself. There *must* be a purpose for all this death. I haven't been witness to all this pain for no reason surely? Bit by bit throughout each event I believe I have been given the opportunity to look at the big picture. I have been lucky enough and honoured enough to be with people that I care about and see them to the other side. I have shared many death journeys with many loving people.

I have been prepared by the Great Creator via a series of death journeys, to go through the worst imaginable event. I have lost my son to death just on the eve of his manhood. I have been ripped off. I do not get to see my baby get his licence, buy his first car, marry the woman of his dreams, settle into his home, enjoy sharing his children. These things will not happen for us Kieran. It is at this point that I have a choice.

I can choose to let the death of a part of my heart overtake me and bring me to my knees. I can give up. Or I can hate. I can hate your friend, the driver of the car, and God or the doctor or people whom are planning happy events for their young men as I write. Or I can think carefully about death and wonder what it means.

I have enough experience in the dead and the dying to make me quite nutty if I choose. In looking deeply at *all* this loss, there must be much to learn. So I thought about it . . . and I searched and I have questioned.

Well my honey, you and I have continued our relationship despite you leaving your body behind. You are just as cheeky and just as impatient and the same caring, loyal son and brother that you were here in your body. With the journey of this last year I have discovered what I suspected as a young nurse working in an old, dark ward in the middle of the night. The dead do not die! They pass to the other side where God resides but we are still loved and still watched over. I know Kieran that you do not miss a trick. I also discovered how excited you were on your anniversary date. You are a great example of how much our loved family and friends keep close to us here on earth. I can at this moment feel your presence as I write this entry. My Reiki hands got hot and you are over my shoulder.

Arriving at this conclusion Kieran, has allowed me to process your death with hope and dignity. I can feel that all is not lost. I can comfort my remaining children and family members with the thought that maybe, just maybe they do not have to say goodbye.

I cannot however, push my views onto our loved ones Kieran but nonetheless they cannot deny some pretty weird contact from you and maybe these thoughts developing in their minds may ease the pain in their hearts. I dearly hope so because apart from losing you Kieran, the next biggest trauma for me is watching the agony of your brothers and sisters. Month after month, your family and dearest friends struggle to find their feet and keep going.

Your poor ole mum

25th July, 2008

There have been many changes in our lives recently Kieran. Our four remaining children now have partners, all of whom we are fond. This means of course that we have also doubled our problem load! More family means more arguments or more illness . . . ! But it also shows me that life will go on. When Tara went out with someone else, I felt left behind with my pain of your loss. I felt that she was over you. However, then I discovered that people did not stop missing you Kieran but simply took their pain with them into the next part of their lives. Tara struggles each day.

My family will grow and we will laugh in our togetherness. And always you will be with us. Which is pretty much what you have been telling me all along! Yes, yes I know . . . I never listen to you! We received a letter from Aimee several weeks ago. She is missing the family and acknowledges her poor choices. She was hoping that perhaps we might consider forgiving her. It was a letter that created confusion and reluctance and for some in our family, anger. We simply did not know how to respond. After several days of chewing it over and being acutely aware that I could not continue this angry blight in my journey, I began to play with the idea of answering her letter.

However, overall there was no time to ponder. Just like that we became grandparents and so the family grew some more. I did get your messages Kieran, that Aimee needed love and so we went to her and we talked things through. With a baby boy's arrival in the world, there can be no place for anger and bitterness. Perhaps this part of my journey has been equally difficult. I shed a flood of tears when making my decision to put pain behind me and welcome a little boy and hug his mother. I remain wary and don't expect Liam, Bridget or Chris to follow my lead as that is their journey, but for me the pain in my heart from losing two children that week has eased. Your heart Kieran is full of love and I can hear you tell me that it is time to let the anger and bitterness go.

Recently I noticed a journal that I had written in some years ago. I wrote in a separate book for each of you children. I felt that a death was imminent and felt that it might have been mine so I began my messages. Yours Kieran, read like this:

"Dear Kieran,
This is a journal of my memories of you and I, and I one day hope to give this to you full of scribble! It is a place where I can write down how cute you were when tiny, how stubborn you are when mad, how giggly you are when tickled! . . . and other such memories including how proud I am of you for all your hard work in battles fought and won. You have striven for personal achievement, and obtained it in many areas of your life, and I have the deepest respect for you for doing so. At this point in time on the first page, Kieran, you are 11 years old and it is October in the year 2000. Tomorrow is Bridget's 8th birthday. I am hoping you will come home for her day, from your dad's at Hallam.

The year 2000 is an interesting year in which to start writing. You will remember no doubt, the amazing parties and fireworks when New Years arrived for the Millennium. You and Bill were with Fran and Dad and you rang us on the mobile phone . . ."Happy New Year!" Lots of people thought all the computers would go down and nothing would work. They had all sorts of emergency strategies in place but amazingly, nothing went wrong! One lady went back to jungle greens and had all sorts of survival tactics in place . . . This year we have also had the Sydney Olympic Games which were hailed as the best ever, then the Para-Olympics . . . fantastic stuff! Only a few years ago disabled people couldn't get support for anything and now finally, recognition for skills and acceptance of ordinary human rights. How slow that change in society has been. For our family, 2000 has been a busy year.

You, Kieran changed schools to a Christian College, going into grade 4 with Miss Pentland whom worked so hard to help you. What a wonderful teacher wasn't she? This year was a big one for holidays – remember our week in Mansfield and the day tobogganing in the snow? You were wet and cold and refused to come in and dry! Watching you flying through the air was very entertaining – so were the landings! I missed you when you flew to N.T. and took your tour to Uluru – I thoroughly loved getting your phone calls every couple of days and I followed your journey on the map after each call."

My journal did not progress very far because I began working back at the hospital with shiftwork and then later as a District Nurse on an average of 50 hours a week. My precious time began to be urgent time. However, my memories linger to and fro about you while we went to Queensland, New Zealand, camping and other little things. The same traits of you stand out in my memory bank Kieran. Your enthusiasm and excitement were at extreme levels on all adventures! Your love of challenges, new things to see and do and your ability to laugh during adversity never faltered! No doubt about it Kieran, you were the best company and so fun loving! You could never sit still for one moment. But then again, you never forgot to stop and put an arm around me and say "Hey Mama!" And of course, you could be damn cranky, Mr Grumpypants!

With so many memories safely encapsulated in my brain, and a long journey of grief to learn from, I have now come to a place where I can see a point to it all. I have learnt about myself and learnt not to judge others. Hang on, *learning* not to judge others. It is a tricky business sometimes!

Sometimes Kieran, it has been the hardest thing to get up and go to work and smile reassuringly at my patients, giving them the care they need and long for. Yet, when I make the effort, they give back more to me than I gave to them!

My patients seem so grateful for the smallest efforts and never forget to check on me if I forget to smile that day. Although they do not know my story, they send love my way by thanking me warmly for my care. Often we hug. I wonder what they would say if they knew how they have been such strength to me!

26th August, 2008

Today I held Malcolm's grandchild in my arms. Aimee's baby boy. An understanding of your words finally entered my head. Yeah, Kieran, you can stop your dramatic clapping! I have always been a mum to the five of you kids and anyone else whom wanted to pop through and be parented for however long. Many young folk have called me mum. My heart has been open.

However, each of these many people have a journey of their own to attend to. I am *not* everyone's mum despite wanting to fix everyone. I love my five dearly but I cannot take away the pains of each child's journey. Aimee has a birth mum and must deal with her the best way she can. Kieran, you have work to do on the other side with God, and I need to understand that God has called you to attend these duties. Your brothers and sisters have their own grief and other problems to work through. With all of you, I begin to see that it is my role to love you, even suggest advice when asked but no longer to fix your problems. I am learning to love without interfering. When there is so much death and pain from loss, I have wanted to shield you all from it. But I can't can I? Learn to love but not take on others' problems you tell me.

Holding little Kristopher set me to thinking that I should feel grateful that Aimee has invited me to hold her baby. She has honoured me with her desire to share her mothering experiences with me and ask my advice, despite our most tragic of past events.

Having you leave me Kieran, in the physical sense, has taught me (be it ever so slowly . . . !) to check each of my relationships and value the positives available and to love each person despite their less endearing traits! I wanted to die when we buried you Kieran. I could not function. My life and my heart stopped. It is nearly 16 months since I held your broken body and said goodbye. Together my beautiful, loving family and I have crawled back from the edge. Each child has needed counselling, has missed exams, failed to get out of bed, screamed with rage, forgotten important dates. It doesn't matter. Each day fighting to get our lives back is a day won. Understanding that you never left us Kieran is central to our healing. You love us and we love you. That will never change. The fact is, God needs you more than we do and that is an honour. You are our Olympian. Our Chosen One. We are learning to live with you watching over us.

4th September, 2008 (Your dad's birthday)
I do need to add here that however much I have come to understand a little of the bigger picture, I am still human. Yesterday I was filled with rage. I think of you hundreds of times a day, even fleetingly, every day. Yesterday I wanted to smash something. I felt so filled with grief and there was nothing I could do to change the simple fact that you will never walk into my kitchen again and throw your arm over my shoulder. Sometimes that knowledge is just *too* big. I paced up and down raging and frustrated. Yet today I feel weepy. What a crazy journey . . . Regardless of what I have learned in the past many months, I will have a lifetime of being a mum whom has

lost a precious son. The days stroll on and we each do the best with what we have and what we know.

Love always,

Mum

10th September, 2008

Yesterday marked 17 months without you. In the big picture, that is no time at all. I have been teary on and off during the week. I think a huge amount of the grieving process is all about coping and the fatigue it causes. The ripples after a catastrophic event still have not settled and in fact take many years before loved ones and friends can claim any sort of normality. This in itself is exhausting but when you have to contain all the emotions and appear well to the outside world, your workmates or school friends, it is so easy to become sick.

All of us tire easily and catch colds more than we did before. The tidal wave effect just keeps rolling on. It is so helpful that in our case we are mostly a very close family and watch over each other. This of course includes you since I *know* you watch over us! Grief is the sort of thing that can tear families apart if effort is not made. It really is huge.

Meantime, I have seen two more Mediums since my last mention and it was interesting to note the exact same use of words by both people claiming to be talking with you. Naturally I chose to hear your messages. Both times you said, "you are not listening, mum . . ." and also "love people just as they are" going on to explain that I can love everyone but I do not need to take on their problems. In fact Kieran, that would make it several times that you have sent messages via different Mediums using your language. You have also sent other people to me when you want to make contact. It has been quite handy because then I get the feeling that I should seek someone whom can "translate" for me over a more relaxed session. For example, remember the day I had a guest who was quite distracted at lunch? Finally she told us that our son was "quite persistent" and later went on to tell us that you asked us to watch Bridget carefully. Sure enough, a few days later Bridget fell down some steps and damaged her ankle ligaments. She was unable to dance and attend her exams for a term. That is a difficult thing for a young dancer looking for a career.

Do you remember the psychic whom wanted to know who "Daniel" is? She said that my son kept saying, "Tell mum 'Daniel' and she will know it is me". Well Kieran, you were right. I did know it was you trying to contact me so after that event I caught up with you in a lovely long session. You were rather cheeky and had the Medium in stiches. So some things just don't change! I guess it is a bit like you are only a phone call away! Except that I do not always have that international dial on.

Today Karen and I took most of your clothes out of the wardrobe in your room and cut them into 8 inch squares. I have a lovely friend, one of our patients at work, whom has agreed to make a quilt out of these squares. I simply was not up to just throwing away your clothes so this is one way I can keep a part of you with us. I can wrap myself in your clothes in winter! I must say though Kieran, that you were not a particularly clean teenager!

We also had a photo frame made up of some dried plants together with some photos of you. There was a mauve rose from your cemetery rose, a leaf from your birthday tree and some dried flowers from your funeral bouquets. The frame looked lovely and went across to your dad for Father's Day.
Little bit by little bit we, which means largely me, are letting go of your material possessions. We sift through sorting out things every few months and are beginning to keep very treasured things. Next to go will be some of your magazines . . . but we will keep the books

you loved. Your Auntie Mandy is building a treasure chest of wood in which to place some of your sacred belongings for us all to peek at from time to time in the future. I know you don't mind what we do with your gear and would like to see them used but it is also important to me that your personality is accessible physically as well as in our memories Kieran. In human terms, it may be a long time before I can move in with you and collect that hug I am after!
I do love you. Mum.

12th September, 2008
Another young life lost yesterday Kieran, and more on the news. God is calling quite a few of you young folk home for Heavenly duties Kieran. I know it must be this way. My heart aches for their families however. I am under no illusion of what is happening within those household walls. May God be with them all and guide them through. I can only hope and pray that they choose wisely how they will cope once the shock dissipates. It is a terrible and heart rendering decision to make.

Shattered hearts never really mend but with healthy choices, it is possible to soothe them. I am deeply saddened that I have come to know this.
Mama.

20th September, 2008
Memories float in as I move around our suburb. I visualised you doing jumps on your new Stumpjumper bike at the wetlands across the road whilst I watched. "Come and watch me jump mum" you called out. It was cold and so, laughing, I took the car to the next street and parked it where I could watch you practice your new and tricky manoeuvres. Your arms and legs were still awkward and coltish. Sometimes you flew through the air with ease and I would

clap and wave. Then again, sometimes I would cringe as I watched you struggle to keep your feet whilst your bike crashed through the undergrowth! Each time you jumped, you would look up and check that I was still there. I would grin and toss you a thumbs up!

I often see you in my mind jumping your skateboard in the driveway over a homemade ramp which kept collapsing at every jump. Still you kept persevering. "Mum, look how much better I am getting at this!" I hear you yell. I would be watching you from the kitchen bench while I peeled potatoes. You seemed so fearless!

Sometimes I enjoy sweet thoughts of past events but often I continue to pick out the regrets. What a useless habit to keep. I wish I would stop it and know that you are frustrated by me continuing to wish I had done differently at whatever event I choose to pick to pieces. I try to tell myself that you understand that I always love you no matter what but my guilt will not ease. Small moments and inconsequential events all are scrutinised and found wanting in my department. I am driving my family crazy, including you.

My health has been suffering over the last few months. I had been back to work for over 15 months but with long hours of giving care to my patients and finding daily struggles at home, I am really exhausted.
Liam had been chronically ill during the year losing a total of 17 kilos although he has managed to battle his way back and Chris struggled to get through his final year of school. I took a month off work several weeks ago but found that I would be needing more than a little rest. I arranged to take a year off work to strengthen both myself and the family.

The first thing I did was pick up your clothes quilt. My lovely friend had actually managed to make two 6 foot x 6 foot quilts from your clothes! They are beautiful and I love them. I am so glad that I did not give your clothes away to the op shop. Bridget can be seen cuddled into one of them and tells me that she can smell you. It is delightfully comforting to have such an item.

I will bet anything that you are rolling your eyes though!

3rd October, 2008

Kieran, you continue to find innovative ways to let us know you are around. I would expect nothing less. At my birthday recently, a special friend of mine presented me with a beautiful gift and told of the peculiar circumstances that caused her to choose it. She told me that upon entering a new age gift store and asking for gift suggestions, she was led to a gorgeous, huge rose quartz. The weird part of her story involved the strange woman whom came up behind her. Denise had never met this lady but, unasked, this same woman offered the advice of "tell your friend to put the quartz alongside the photos of her son". Interestingly, the family on the day of my birthday, had given to me a digital photo frame with continuous photos of you Kieran, and I had not had the opportunity to tell anyone. Feeling you around me Kieran has become second nature and I do not question it.

As for the family, they all soldier on but with nowhere near the energy that they once had. They do not reach as high for their goals but I guess as time passes, that too will change.

Aimee is visiting for the first time next week, bringing with her the baby and her partner. It is my hope that this will be a healing time for all but it is not for me to fix everything. (I trust you notice this bit Kieran!) Anxiety and wariness roam around the house a little however, but we will sort this out as we always do.

As for Daniel, the driver of the vehicle that you were crushed beneath, he is trying to cope with the Laws that are enforced in our country. We have been told that the Court Case is only months away. All of us, including both fathers sincerely hope that his sentence is minimal. Both men have managed to find a place of peace in regards to Daniel although they have no wish to see him. The consequences for Daniel are lifelong ones and my heart aches for him.

8th December, 2008

Aimee stayed for a couple of weeks and we managed to sort out a great deal. She was humble and quiet, demanding nothing. Her siblings have been watchful with her Kieran but this is something that she quietly accepts. Aimee has made it clear to me that she has no right to expect forgiveness but simply hopes that one day it may arrive. I hope so too.

I have spent much time being a support to Aimee and teaching her what I know about caring for babies. I asked her what she wanted from me and she asked if I would consider being both her mother and Kristopher's grandmother. She chatted to me about her mistakes in going back to Portland and about her recent lessons in life. Having the baby around eases things a little and gradually, slowly the family extend to her a little of the Family Code. Love us and respect us and we shall return the same. It is a wary start.

By way of moving on, I have been studying Natural Health. I am learning Kinesiology, ongoing Reiki and Australian Bush Flower Essences. Guess what the essence of Macrocarpa (one of the flowering gums) is used for Kieran? It is used to give energy and encourage rest. It is taken at times of great physical stress when endurance is necessary. Macrocarpa is a great remedy for people who are recuperating to strengthen their adrenal glands. No surprise there!

Mum

10th February, 2009

It has been a long time since I have written but I chat to you each day and send you prayers every night. We made it through another Christmas, this time staying firmly at home. I asked that everyone be here for an early lunch then they were free to go anywhere they liked. This worked out very well and enabled us to toast you Kieran and spend time together and then your brothers and sisters were off to the homes of their partners. Mal and I visited you in the cemetery for a long and comfortable time on our own after lunch.

Aimee spent many weeks with us again through January and my time was invested in renewing our relationship and all of us getting to know Kris. He was starting to become more interesting as he developed his personality and could often be found in someone's bedroom being dressed up, teased or played with. The poor kid hasn't got a hope with this lot!

January was also a time of emotional turmoil as I prepared myself to write a Victim Impact Statement for the prosecution. A couple of months ago Martin, Mal and I had sat in on a meeting regarding the details of Daniel and your court case. We were invited to say whatever we wished to in our statements.

After great thought by all the family (everyone was invited to say something), I was the only one to decide I would write up a statement. It was on my mind a great deal. By now the court had already gone through the processes of Plea hearings and the Final Hearing was set for 25th March. Daniel has been charged with dangerous driving causing death and exceeding both the alcohol levels and recommended speed. He has already been without his licence for a while. However, you were also in charge of your destiny, my honey. Staying in the cab would have saved your life. The Police and Prosecution had been wonderful with us and kept us up to date. We are to be met by a member of the Police at the court on the expected date and all would be explained to us. We cannot complain about our treatment by anyone. We have been looked after the entire way.

Meantime, your mate Mick has kept in touch with me since you left. We have enjoyed many a coffee and chat over these months. He has found it very difficult without your friendship and struggled with many an issue. I cried one evening following one of his spontaneous visits when I could feel him missing you. It was a sharp ache and I knew he was lonely for his best mate. If you had been available, I deeply believe that the two of you would have had your swags in your Ute and been on your way to a new adventure outback.

You had grown into a fine man Kieran with a hardworking ethic and where there was a job to do, you would be found in the thick of it. I can look out of my kitchen window and see Kingi's patio remembering you perched on our fence with hammer in hand. You smiled down at me, happy to have a place in the team of builders and glad to be able to assist Kingi. You learnt how to look another man in the eye, shake his hand and offer your help. That was the core of Kieran Browne. Not bad son, for a lad with struggles in sight, hearing, coordination and social expectation! You overcame so much, including anger and even drugs.

Many people came to tell us of stories about you helping them with this and that. I have letters from strangers in country towns informing us of your good deeds. I am not surprised. Mal and I had mentioned to each other what a fine person you were becoming. My personal favourite memory is of you taking me out for tea with your first wage! You drove me (on your learner's permit) up the mountains to The Pine Grove Bistro. We talked and enjoyed a lovely meal. You told me about the business you wanted to develop as a one stop vehicle maintenance shop. Later you drove me down to another cafe where we ate ice-cream. I was so touched that you gave me this lovely gesture and when I thanked you, telling you how much I had enjoyed our night, you mentioned that you hoped we could do it again. Unfortunately we never did. I wish you could have been here longer with us. I would have loved to see you build on your dreams.

15th February, 2009

The Flowering Gum continues in an unexpected way. It is 21 months later and I have presented to you a story of sorts amongst the cathartic outpourings of my maternal despair. Again however, I find myself at a huge stalemate and filled with despondency. Do I have depression Kieran? . . . probably. Is that normal? . . . probably. I laugh and sing, encourage my children and enjoy my grandchild. I have a basic plan for my future in regards to moving on in my nursing role. I want to give something to the community and use my knowledge in a supportive and caring way. I am not glued to a lounge chair dribbling over a TV set and I am active. I study and go to the gym. I clean my house and enjoy coffee with friends. The family seem strong and functioning, now making healthy decisions for their future and I can step into the background. For the most part, they are fine and will make it through life as independent, kind and loving people with an awareness of how precious life is and also how precarious. They have also worked out the difference between *real* friends and those that just take. My children are in fact, more sane and balanced than I am.

Which brings me back to my original thought! I am uncertain right now where I stand in the world or even where I want to stand. I really just feel utterly exhausted. I have to admit finally that I have given away my energy to others and forgot to save some for me! What is the secret to loving, sharing and guiding but keeping a shield around yourself so that you can remain unaffected? Did Mother Theresa cuddle everyone then rush home to cry or did she pat everyone and wander home to pizza with a glass of wine over a good book? How does one care and assist from the heart in the time of need of another and not be affected in some way? If you block out the emotion of the needs, then you bypass the incoming lessons of life. If you open to these lessons, then you run the risk of burn out. What is the balance to this dilemma? Now take the dilemma and add your own grief, and figure that out!

OK. I am exhausted but it all still comes back to your basic message to me. I have overshot in the caring department! Since I am weary but not old enough to die yet, then I obviously have many more things to learn! God isn't going to swing past with a million dollars and tell me that it is my turn to hang from a hammock with a pina colada in the Bahamas for the next 20 years. Bugger!

So then, since I have more things to deal with ahead of me, I had better batten down the hatches, wrap my protective shawl around myself and think about boundaries. With a court case on my doorstep, I will need to give some care to me. Are you impressed? With love, your clever mum!

June 2009

Well what do you know, time has shot past me again! I am amazed that the last three months of incredible events have finally eased. One minute I was busily studying Flower Essences and attending school for Kinesiology and the next minute all hell broke loose!

Let me tell you about the court case first Kieran. I sent off the Victim Impact Statement (see pages 166 to 168) giving an overview of our real life situation and also my hope that Daniel be given the opportunity to get on with his life and recover without a jail term. Our family agreed with this sentiment Kieran but it was incredible how many people in general were disturbed by the concept of Daniel getting off with a minimal term. Over and over again we were questioned on our thoughts, as if we had gone mad.

The facts of the matter come back to two things. Firstly, Daniel has been traumatised by your death and his experience with it. Our belief is that he has learnt a hard lesson without jail. Secondly, whatever happens to Daniel, we will not have you returned to us. The outcome changes nothing in our lives. On the other side of the same coin, we risk bitterness and hatred by hoping for heavy punishment. I am pleased to say that my family are forgiving enough and loving enough to let things be. Life teaches lessons so who are we to cast stones. I do not say this lightly Kieran. It has not been an easy road.

Following two court sessions during the last week of March and the first week of April, the Judge of the County Court in Melbourne finally declared a sentence. With a great deal of thought and compassion including strong leanings towards my Impact Statement, he sentenced Daniel to 18 months jail term with a 15 month suspension, granting Daniel with a short stop of only three months. Mal, Liam and I had attended quietly on the side for the sentencing and were approached by Daniel's Mum who took me in her arms and cried. My Iron Will specially built for court proceedings dissolved and the two of us shared a moment as tormented mums. I sincerely wish his family healing and love as they follow their own road which will be a different one to ours but also difficult.

I was extremely thrown however, when I was phoned the same evening by Daniel's family to tell me that the newspapers had our story and would run it in the morning. I was having trouble getting my head around the day's details and I could not quite understand why the case would make a state newspaper. However, the next morning they ran the story and Bridget was most indignant that you were referred to as the "dead man". It upset her no end. I was troubled by the newspaper involvement but imagine it must be way worse for Daniel and his own. For our family, it is over.

Before I had time to mull this over, Easter arrived upon us again and brought with it more disaster. Your Aunty Mandy had developed an inflamed breast that resisted treatment and I raced down to her country town to join her for further tests. It looked like an aggressive and rare form of breast cancer. She was given a date with a senior Oncologist at Peter McCallum Hospital in Melbourne city and it was arranged that she stay with us and also join in our family Kieran-Anniversary on the 9th and then Good Friday on the 10th. As usual, anniversary times are stressful and again we stopped to think of you from Monday to Thursday as your dates of coma until dying . . . then again, straight into Good Friday until Easter Monday. A whole week back to back of anniversary. That should have been exhausting enough.

However, the week became worse. Mandy and I drove from the country to the city for her appointment. The news they imparted was grim. On her first diagnosis, Mandy was told that she was already a stage 4 breast cancer patient with liver metastasis. There would be no treatment but chemotherapy would be given to prolong life. We drove home in silence. She was greeted by your two cousins Kieran, still teenagers whom had already lost a father to cancer. David must be tearing his hair out up there with you Kieran.

After thinking about it all overnight, Mandy asked me to tell the boys. I took them for a drive and shared this difficult news only a few hours before we had a group of family arriving for a small dinner to remember you Kieran. I have to say that it was an emotional and tumultuous meal with mixed thoughts roaming around. On the one hand we were trying to send a cheery hello to you Kieran and on the other, we were all in shock and bumbling around. I cannot begin to imagine how bizarre it must have been for Mandy and the boys to be toasting you and then trying to imagine a hollow future. It would have been better to cancel the dinner and I know you would have understood Kieran but this night just evolved by itself. Pop and Shirley had recently arrived from New Zealand and your cousin Bonnie wanted to acknowledge you and see Pop at the same time. They are really lovely and I feel honoured that they wish to expand the family get togethers. Somehow the night grew to 19 people. On the other hand, it gave Mandy the perfect opportunity to talk to her family and collect her hugs. Where would we be without each other?

Easter came and went with another three hour trip to the country to take Mandy home and a visit to see you at "your place". We find it tricky getting through the many days of remembrance. Mandy was to have a "normal" week which by now included massive pain and no sleep. She was finding it hard. However in the true spirit of the proverbial battler, she got right to the business of educating herself and finding solutions. Together we sat and nutted out her pain control issues, having them ready to check with her specialist on the next visit. We worked out a series of natural therapies to add to the medical plan and discussed what tactical thoughts we would employ. It was not difficult to agree that neither Mandy nor I would accept a negative result. In fact we had told the Oncologist that we were only accepting positive behaviour and plans. The Oncologist had given us a small smile and simply nodded. There is always a solution of sorts to every issue.

I was then to be off to the country again to accompany her back to the city for her first chemotherapy in a few days' time.

Aimee, Matt and Baby Kris arrived to visit for a fortnight at this time. They were toying with the idea of moving closer to us and I was looking forward to catching up and cuddling Kris. Pop and Shirley had also arrived for a holiday and were flying around spending time with as many of the family as they could. It was a busy household and must have been overwhelming for Mandy at times.

Bridget meantime, had been struggling with delayed depression all of the year. As a teenager, it can be normal to delay grief until one is older and can think it through a bit more. Bid was having trouble keeping up with everything and was putting off both her dance classes and school. I was seriously becoming concerned, although I had been expecting a belated reaction to the many deaths that the children were all struggling to come to terms with.

I have learnt that if I am feeling fatigued from coping then somehow everyone in the house experiences the same sensation to some degree. It is a strange phenomenon but it basically means that none have of us are completely up and running . . . . and perhaps we never will be entirely.

A day before I was to collect Mandy, I took a phone call. "This is the Metropolitan Ambulance. I am ringing to tell you that your husband Malcolm has just been hit by a car and we are taking him to the Alfred Hospital. This is the hospital with the best trauma facilities in the state."

I sat down in a daze. Unbelievable!

Mal was conscious and had managed to warn the ambulance drivers about you and the family aversion to the Alfred Hospital. The hospital itself is fine of course but by association we would rather like to avoid it! However, as per many of my life experiences, when God wants me to get over something, He does not muck around.

As gently as I could, I told Bid that Dad had been through a little accident. I watched as her eyes glazed over. Without a word she stood and drifted across to her bed. She climbed in, snuggled into a comfortable position and pulled the quilt over her head. She refused to leave her bed for the following three days. I had no words to comfort her with.

It is a testament to this family that Liam and Chris arranged a cup of tea and a bite to eat before they drove me into the hospital. The two of them joked around and we laughed as we do. Sorry Mal but we were hungry!

On arrival at the hospital, we found the side doors closed but alongside was a card swiping device for staff to get inside with. In shenanigans that are typical of all you boys in our family, both Chris and Liam began to devise ways to get in without walking the long distance to the front door of the hospital. "I have my I.D. card" began Liam and proceeded to swipe it. The door failed to open. "No, no . . . this is an old run down hospital . . . they want money so we need to try a credit card," Chris determined. Still the door ignored us. "No man, they won't take credit" and Liam tried his bank card. Having this fail, they were both excited about their next idea.

"Hey, this is a *hospital*! The door will open if we use a *Medicare* card!". I waited while they tried to swipe each of their Medicare cards and patiently wondered what security was making of all this via the camera just above our heads! It sometimes appears that I travel with my very own circus but I *really* love my Clowns! So inevitably, we began the long walk around the block to the front door of the dreaded hospital to see what poor ole Mal was up to in the Emergency Department.

Mal had been riding his road bike home from work when he was struck by a young driver coming through a roundabout from the other side. He was already halfway across when she ran into him and was thrown onto her bonnet. He suffered a severe concussion, a lung contusion, five fractured ribs and a well and truly broken scapula. It was another three months before he could return to work four hours a week . . . . with the knowledge that the young driver was suing for the cost of her bonnet!

So my lovely Kieran, our lives, yours and mine became a series of hospitals, appointments, country drives and counselling. The boys helped out when they could, sometimes driving me around. Liam refused to let me drive Mandy home on one occasion due to my fatigue, and escorted us both. I could feel your concern and constant presence Kieran. It was comforting to know that you were there. When Mal finally arrived home from hospital sleep, already in short supply for both of us, became non-existent. If I thought I was tired before, then I was tricking! *Now* I'm really tired! The last three months have been hard.

Aimee stayed for a few weeks helping me by looking after your dad while I went with Mandy to her treatments. I would stay with her and the boys for a few days each time to help out as she felt so very ill but I could not spend too much time away from Malcolm.

Mal was unable to sleep for more than short bursts due to extreme pain and lived in the lounge chair. I dozed in bed getting up and down to nurse him. It was many weeks later before he even tried sleeping in bed and even then he needed to be sleeping upright. Meanwhile Mandy had all sorts of horrific responses to her chemotherapy including severe chest pain and shortness of breath—even turning blue! There had been an extremely difficult day when both Mal and Mandy experienced emergency situations at the same time! While I sat with Mandy as she commenced her chemotherapy, she began to gasp for breath with chest pain and the staff rushed toward her with the emergency trolley and oxygen. Not to be outdone, over in another hospital, Mal also began to experience chest pain and panicked the staff with Atrial Fibrillation. I was called and found myself in the awkward situation of seeing Mandy stabilised and then flagging down a taxi and rushing to the Alfred Hospital some forty five minutes away to ensure that Mal was being stabilised!

Obviously they both survived but by the end of the day I was wondering just how *my* poor weary heart had survived! . . . . however, despite these frightening experiences, Mandy has persevered and now overall, her lesions are smaller. She hopes to improve on this and keep the lesions in shrunken form indefinitely. For Mandy, a decision had to be made. It is a personal choice on whether one will continue to fight or give up. I have watched her envelop herself with a lovely mix of medical treatment and holistic assistance. She tries it all with a healthy dose of hope. So far we are reaping the benefits. This journey of hers continues. She now has her treatments in her country town and has various people in place to assist. I try and drive down every three weeks just to annoy her and make a bit of trouble!

Mal managed to trip his heart into a new type of arrhythmia due to the severe pain that he suffered. His past heart problem had been behaving for a while now but there you go. There is always an issue to care about. He will be a long time in healing but again, we travel forward at a manageable pace and take it as it comes.

Bridget is bravely churning along and getting herself back on track. We bought her a debutante dress for her ball next week and can't wait to see her looking stunning. Aimee has never experienced a formal or Deb so Bridget bought her a beautiful dress to attend the ball in. Both girls have shared bookings for hair and makeup with the intention of doing sister things. They are both excited. This will likely be Aimee's only shot at being a teenager for the duration because she is newly pregnant again. We all handled the news with more grace this time!

Life goes on . . . .
Time stops for no man as the saying goes. We all grow accustomed to living within the boundaries of our pains and demons. It becomes easier to go forward and adjust to new ideas and future plans. Liam has bought, renovated and moved into a cute unit and plans his career moves. Chris too continues his studies toward architecture.

Mal has not healed well and struggles with continual shoulder issues. I am becoming very skilled at back massage!

Nonetheless, recently with terrible shock and sadness, I was shot back into the past . . . and into a new grief.

My beautiful niece Bonn introduced a young man into our lives some years ago and we came to love Ben as a fun-loving but caring, sensitive man. He was with us in our journey of losing you Kieran, and gave me the warmest hug. As he did so, he expressed to me how terrible it must be to lose a child and hoped his parents never had to experience this. Unfortunately, Ben died as result of a diving accident just weeks ago. I so wish his family did not have to take this journey. To his loved ones and our Bonnie, I can only send love and a deep understanding.

Just to remind me that you are around and aware of all the events going on, it was at this time of aching for Ben that a clear message from you arrived. I was quietly ironing with the radio running in the background with some sort of general type music. Without warning my stomach clenched and I stopped what I was doing. With a heavy frown I wondered what had grabbed my "attention". I became aware that a song was playing on the radio. With undisputable surety I knew that you were around Kieran. The song playing was "*I Will Always Love You* . . ." but this time, it was sung by a male and I had never heard this older version. I felt a little teary at the notion of you playing me a beautiful song and the tears began to drip down my cheeks. I couldn't help but feel a little bit rebuked when as clear as a bell, I heard you say . . . *Awww Mum, don't start the tears* . . . !! With that, I gave a slightly embarrassed chuckle, wiped my eyes and settled back to listen to this lovely song.

What sort of comment do you think a DJ might conclude a loving song with folks? Perhaps he might mention lovers, or a past movie or wish everyone a nice life . . . However, the DJ jolted me hard with his throw-away line. "That was Dolly Parton and Vince Vaughn. Don't let your son catch you crying!"

Don't let your son catch you crying???? OK Kieran, I got that message loud and clear! I love you too and I am getting less teary! It is so nice that the messages keep arriving to reinforce all I am learning and what I have yet to discover.

Obviously I will not be headed back to work for a while but my studies are again a part of my life. I have seen Colin from the Grief and Bereavement Centre a few times. I was chatting to him about my thoughts of a different life and in particular, moving on from nursing at some point. He very wisely told me that my life has changed. It will never be the same again. I cannot go back to where I was nor whom I was. So I guess it is *forward ho* . . .

I am growing up Kieran!

Mum xxx

3rd July, 2009

Today Daniel will return home from his time in prison. His three months are now behind him. He will be released back to his family. I imagine in my private vision that he reaches towards his mother in their reunion, her arms outstretched as he envelopes her. She wraps her arms around his waist and leans her head upon her son's chest as she cries her tears of relief, sheds her aches for her boy.

How do I feel about this? I feel dull and jaded. Old before my time. I wish this vision were me.

If I close my eyes and imagine, I can still feel your arms around me. Your chin rests on my head. Your lips touch my cheek.

I know you are with me, around me, watching over me. I am bruised and broken. Despite my rehabilitation there will always be scars that never heal. I wish you were coming home arms out-stretched but I count myself lucky that your presence is felt.

Do I still believe I did the right thing in supporting Daniel, wishing him well on his journey? Yes I do. I cannot live with both grief and anger. Grief is enough on it's own.

My beautiful Kieran, my second born son, I wait with interest to see what wonderful messages you will send to us as time scoots by. We continue to learn how to cope with tragedy and benefit from its sad messages. Daily we send our prayers of love to you and ask that you hear us. We have great faith and a deep belief that you do and that one day we shall be together again. It is soothing to know this despite it being a long wait.

Our family has been blessed because we have each other and we have you. Thank you for your love. I might say here too, thanks for your fun and sometimes crazy messages! Some things just don't change! Thank God for that!

I look forward to our continued growth and loving relationship together. I love you endlessly.
Mama.

EPILOGUE

Despite the details of this one family and the repercussions of a loved one's death, it must be acknowledged that Loss is a part of life. Death is inevitable. It is the dream of what you might want your life to be that is shattered when you lose a loved one. (Not to mention the turmoil and worry of wondering how your loved one is faring.) I had dreamt of seeing all of my babies happy and successful with babies of their own. I wanted to witness the results of my parenting. People whom lose partners wanted to grow old together, maybe finally travel the world together . . . many dreams are destroyed when losing a precious one. Of course, there are those that lose several loved ones in a single foul swoop. What a devastation that would be.

Yet, nothing happens by chance. The Creator, whomever or whatever you perceive Him to be has orchestrated these events long before they happen. Sometimes the wisdom is brought to earth beforehand as was the case with our Kieran. He *knew* he would not be here long and he made sure he experienced life as fully as possible because of this. I have read of others whom have known in advance what their destiny is to be. There are also many, many documented cases of contact with our loved ones on the other side. I am no Medium or clairvoyant. I have simply known many deaths. With this awareness I have been able to watch for messages. They come with regularity. Often in a way that is otherwise inexplicable. It is not frightening. The souls of the people we love exist and are the same as when they were here with us in body. Anyone can receive the loving messages that are on offer.

Feel good about sending prayers and loving messages to your loved one each day. They will be received with joy. Providing the reaching out to the other side is done with pure love and good intent, all will be well. My journey has taught me that there are many lovely spirits looking out for each one of us. They cannot make your choices for you but you can ask them for assistance, guidance, and love. What a great support as we travel the rocky road of life.

It has also been a part of my journey to understand that the Great Creator does not give more pain than one can bear. It often feels like it of course. For the person being challenged by a loss, you *can* survive. We can ask for help and it does arrive.

For the person being challenged by the possibility of losing your life, you still have choices. Choose to fight back or not. Choose to find solutions to the many issues or not. Choose to understand that your challenge is for your Higher learning. What will you do with this information? It is your choice. None of us are alone. Ask for help.

Grief, of course, encompasses all sorts of issues including your own poor health, abuse by someone close to you, broken trust . . . the list is long. Needless to say, love and healthy choices will help with all of them.

Everyone has a time of grief in their life. All losses are to be grieved over and all grief offers opportunity to learn. One cannot have life without death. Or joy without pain, or success without loss. To know when you are lucky, you must know what it is to be without. To find out how fickle and petty humans can be, one must experience an important loss. Most important in all of this, is the giving of love. Why learn all of these things if you are only going to shut life out and become cold? Loving is living. The greatest gift to others and the greatest way to heal yourself is to love.

I must confess a fascination with the Native American view of life as it was lived in the past. It contains deep respect for Life, Death, Mother Earth and each other. I fully recommend reading *Earth Dance Drum*, A Celebration of Life by Blackwolf and Gina Jones Published by Commun-a-key in Salt Lake City. A chapter on grief highlights some simple truths.

"Honour yourself when you experience grief.

To define loss is to insult the griever, for there are no limits to the losses in life. No-one can really know what it is like to be you and to lose what you have lost. Your relationship with a lost person or experience is unique to you. Your grief is also unique. No one can enter that place of grief. Do not expect them to enter. Do not ask them to enter. Do not wish them to enter. For it is meant for you alone. Although others cannot enter, they may grieve alongside you. Loss can be the great storm that brings the clouds together."

The message of this beautiful and helpful book relates that everyone will know grief. When your turn arrives know that you are not alone and that all of life will experience the tears of loss.
Everyone, too, will have their loved ones not that far away and without question waiting to be acknowledged!

Take heart in the fact that despite life being turned upside down and inside out, we will adapt and scrabble forward . . . and on our knees is just fine! Keep going and one day we begin to stand, perhaps when we least expect it. Don't forget to "*remember*" that our loved ones will not leave us. They have not gone from us but merely gone before us. Meantime, find your tree and hang on tight!

THE END

VICTIM IMPACT STATEMENT of Alexandra
Browne-Hill in reference to the death of Kieran
Shae Browne on 9th April, 2007.

As the mother of 17 year old Kieran at the time of his death, I would
have to say that the ripples of such a huge rock thrown into our little
pond have spread far and wide, more in proportion to a tidal wave. It
is to be expected I guess, because losing a young life is every parents'
worst nightmare.

In our house, I had five wonderful children all striving to find their
way through life and all working towards healthy productive lives.
They were aged between 21 and 14. I carry great pride toward them
for in the 18 months prior to Kieran's death, they had each already
carried the losses of four other loved people including an uncle and
a step-parent to suicide. They coped with dignity and strength.
Following the accident of Daniel and Kieran, these same children
stepped up to deal with the situation of seeing their brother in a
coma for four days and nights. They were present during all events
including last rites and finally seeing their dead brother in hospital
to say goodbye. They coped with funerals and burials. They were
back to their lives within three weeks.

Looking back over the last 20 months I see that there were small
traumas, like the isolation of people withdrawing from us as they
did not know what to say to us about everyone's biggest nightmare,
and then the normal strange processes of grief. Then there were the
horrific traumas. Our eldest son Liam (and Kieran's closest sibling),
over the first six months post event, lost 17 kilos and was finally
unable to move off his bed. Due to the fact that Liam has a cardiac
condition, his GP frantically tried medical help first and even sent
him for a full body scan thinking of cancer. I thought I would lose
another son. When finally he was treated for depression, it took

another six months to regain his health and some of his previous zest for life.

Our third son Chris was attempting his V.C.E. and was unable to concentrate. He roamed around unable to remember a thing . . . I mean more than normal! . . . and cried a lot. Another depression diagnosis. His results were predictably poor but he has now found an enjoyable course of study. Our eldest daughter Aimee at 16 ran away on the Easter weekend of Kieran's "departure" and refused any help. She left behind a hairdressing apprenticeship. We did not see her again until August 2008 when she phoned from the Portland Labour Ward and asked if I could come to help her to deliver her baby. Shock and tears all round! She too is being treated for depression and post trauma. She has grown up and come home but in her own words, stated that she couldn't take any more death. Our youngest child Bridget, at 14, denied any loss until last September when finally growing up got too hard. She is an Honours dance student after 13 years of dancing and last September at 16, she was unable to dance and unable to cope with school despite being, in the previous year, an A grade student. A local psychologist diagnosed her with severe depression and severe anxiety.

My husband Malcolm battles constantly to maintain household normality. He helps the boys with their cars and boy things, and shows extra attention to the girls when needed. He is a wonderful grandfather. However, he is exhausted from watching all our backs and picking us up when we are down.

Me? After nursing for nearly 30 years, my heart has gone out of the nursing game. I gave my last heartfelt nursing to my son in the Alfred Trauma Centre. I went back to my workplace in a daze and I try to give good care but I am exhausted. The children were unable to stand me grieving and I became careful to hide my grief. Supporting and nursing my remaining children became my only goal. When finally my doctor diagnosed fibromyalgia episodes, coeliac disease and mild depression, she offered me six months leave. I am currently on this leave and will need to consider what new career I can manage both physically and emotionally.

We are all okay. The journey has been horrific, full of nightmares both literal and otherwise. However, we are a close family. We support each other and know that the pain will ease a little eventually. We have all learnt many things and refuse to carry any bitterness. Our children truly are our blessings. Our lives will go on and we will make Kieran proud.

Despite everything, our hearts go out to Daniel and Tash, along with their families. A weekend of fun with close friends was not supposed to go like this. We have no anger toward Daniel. Just sadness! He cared about Kieran and has learned about responsible behaviour in the most traumatic and painful way possible. It would be my greatest wish that Daniel and his wife be given the opportunity to go on with their lives and make amends by leading wholesome, happy and responsible lives together, teaching their own children what it means to lose a friend. One ruined family is plenty and surely some good has to come out of my baby giving up his opportunity to live his life and give me his children to hold. I know that Kieran has made an enormous statement to young people because I am often told so by many young adults whom remember him. I am hearing that Daniel's lessons are being shared by many. It makes a little sense in a senseless situation . . . despite those ripples . . .

Alex Browne-Hill
February 7, 2009

Acknowledgments

Most journeys involve other people. This one has been shared by hundreds of wonderful people. To all of those whom stopped their lives to comfort us and share our pain, we are deeply honoured. Kieran would have been flabbergasted at the impact he made on so many people. His philosophy in life was a simple one.

Give a hand when needed and cuddle those that look like they need it . . . Oh and don't forget to fight for the underdog! (This lead Kieran into a few situations!) Needless to say, there were many friends to see Kieran off.

The sensational staff of the Emergency Services, the Victorian Police, the Ambulance Service and the Alfred Hospital along with other wonderful helpers, all deserve a special mention for repeatedly going above and beyond the call of duty. We are indebted to you all.

In the writing of this journey, I send my warmest thanks to my Grief Counsellor Colin for challenging me to write and then to offer my thoughts to others. Colin, you make a difference to the world.

Thanks must go to Samantha for hours of deciphering my scribble and an inspiring belief that we had something to offer the aching heart. Sam, this journal was not possible without you.

In differing ways, so many beloved people have made our grief more bearable. My parents Beth and Clive and their partners Pat and Shirley, my brother Harry and sister Mandy, my work mates, my dearest friends Pauline, Katarina, Denise, Anne, Annette, Catrina, Lisa, Glenda, Nicole and Lesley all played a part in seeing me through. Our neighbours and most special friends the Horuas walked with us step by step as they always do and provided us with an inbuilt support system. There are not enough words to cover the help you have given to us.

Many thanks go to Katarina, Karen and Marilyn for editing, tears and all! There are so many wonderful friends whom have supported us selflessly and we send our love to you all.

Never least is my beloved family. I feel such pride in my children for battling through the biggest trial in their young lives. Liam, Chris, Bridget and yes, Aimee, you have all approached the loss of your brother with courage and dignity. You have carried your journey with determination and love. The support you have given me has brought me to tears often, for always you noticed how I felt and offered hugs unconditionally. In particular is the love and support you give to each other regardless of any circumstances. I am proud to call you my children and delight in our lovely relationship. I welcome to our family all of your partners and hope you each enjoy being a part of it.

To Liam, a special thank you and hug for IT and marketing along with your deep faith and pride in my journey of writing. Your comment of "about time!" struck a chord and got me going!

To my husband Malcolm, a humble thank you for always supporting my ventures regardless of how weird I must seem sometimes! The children refer to you as the Rock and the name truly fits. Nobody gives love and hugs like you do. Quietly you worked to keep the family together when times got tough. Yes, we noticed! We love you!

Finally to Kieran. You have worked hard to stay in touch as promised. We are so lucky to have you in our lives. Thank you for your love and loyalty. We love you too!

Mum

DO NOT STAND AT MY GRAVE AND WEEP

Do not stand at my grave and weep;
I am not there. I do not sleep.
I am a thousand winds that blow.
I am the diamond glints on snow.
I am the sunlight on ripened grain.
I am the gentle autumn rain.
When you awaken in the morning's hush
I am the swift uplifting rush
Of quiet birds in circled flight.
I am the soft stars that shine at night.
Do not stand at my grave and cry;
I am not there. I did not die.

Mary Frye

As read by Grandma Beth at the burial of Kieran – 17th April, 2007

Spoken at the funeral by Martin . . .

I'm making a sweeping assumption that everyone here knew . . . or knew of my son Kieran . . . that he spoke with you, rode with you, lied to you, drank with you, fought with you, loved you, influenced you and was influenced by you . . .

Kieran loved life and could never get enough . . . enough lasagne, enough Bundy, enough excitement, enough thrills, enough fun, enough mates, enough love . . .

If you believe this then we are all here for the same purposes . . .

So before I go on, let me ask you all to spend a short time just to think . . . this time not of Kieran, because I'll get to that . . . but; on this afternoon . . .

Where should you be? What should you be doing? What's on television now? Shouldn't you be on the phone talking to someone? . . . or MySpace or MSNChat swapping gossip . . . planning for the next big night out?

What would you like to be doing just about now? Because you shouldn't be here . . . none of us should be; there is no excitement or fun or loving in death . . . nor in mourning the passing of my son . . .

I can't bear a grudge or demand revenge or even point a finger of blame for this senseless waste of Kieran's life . . . I can get angry, very angry . . . and I have done over the past week . . . but what can I do with it? What good can possibly come from this?

Well . . . nothing really I suppose . . . but while I have you here I'm asking you to listen, really listen and try to understand the simple things I feel I have to say . . . if not for me, then for Kieran because believe it or not there were times when he would ask and I would answer . . . and there were times my answers made a difference . . .

Just no more . . .

Every 17 year old boy thinks he's bullet-proof . . . unstoppable, full of life, out for the next thrill . . . live fast, die fast and leave a good looking corpse . . .

Kieran was born 13th June, 1989

Kieran missed his 18th birthday by two months and four days . . . well eight days really but we'll get to those missing four days . . . the four days where he didn't "die fast" and certainly didn't "leave a good looking corpse" . . .

"It's the quality not the quantity that matters" . . . yeah sure . . . but there has to be a break even point . . . for all his adventures and fast life

Kieran will never get his driver's licence;

Kieran will never own a four wheel drive Ute;

Kieran will never get to Western Australia or work in the mines . . . never again will he throw his swag beside a stream and sleep under the stars . . .

Kieran will never get married;

Kieran will never hold my grand child in his arms and sing sweet melodies . . . *Only the good die young*" . . . well we could debate that one . . .

Kieran always meant well, but there were times when it seemed that he was very good at being bad . . .

Kieran is a likely lad . . . he's had a few nicknames over the years but . . . recently in his B&S phase . . . he earned "Kelpie" and I need to believe it was for all the right reasons because a kelpie pup will nip at your heals, work hard all day and still have time to play and cause trouble . . . all the while showing loyalty and trust . . .

Kieran was trapped under the vehicle for more than an hour . . . with the full weight of it draining the life from him . . . and still he fought on . . .

Everyone that he touched . . . or touched him in those terrible four days fought long and hard for him . . . they ran miles to phone for help, they freed him from the wreck, they gave him emergency care, they flew him to the best hospital, they treated him, washed him, kissed him, nurtured him, gave him themselves until even the hardest trauma care specialists were brought to tears . . . and Kieran fought on . . . his extended family at his side . . .

I believe he knew we were there with him, hoping, praying, cheering him on in his greatest battle . . .

Liam spoke with him and joy of joys he opened his eyes . . .

His nurse asked him to move his tongue so she could clear his mouth and that was right up Kieran's alley as he dutifully but defiantly poked out his tongue . . . past swollen and bloodied lips . . .

We would sit for hours by his side holding his hand, caressing his hair, watching him, talking to him, singing, reading, crying, praying, begging for him just to squeeze a hand one more time . . .

We got practical . . . his mother and I, we split shifts to make sure Kieran's "home-base" was always with him . . . and that we would be strong enough to keep up with his demands as he recovered . . .

I cried that night, I had to leave . . . and was terrified but knew Kieran would improve and stay the night with his mother and Malcolm . . .

In my emotional state I believe Kieran's grandfather shouted at me for my foolishness . . ."He's not ready, not yet . . ."

. . . still I didn't sleep that night . . . and my headache got worse . . .

My boy had a massive bruise on his right buttock . . . like his God had decided to give him a swift kick to wake him up to the facts of life and the rules for living . . . the bruising got worse and poisoned his poor weakened body . . . even though he had used almost his weight in blood products . . . Kieran fought on . . . the doctors, nurses and carers never faltered and surged ahead trying to give my boy even the slightest glimmer of hope to fight . . . and Kieran fought on . . .

His physical heart faltered after days of over 120 beats per minute . . .

120 beats per minute . . . over such a long time even for a 17 year old boy is like running multiple marathons end on end . . . and Kieran fought on . . .

You should choose the fights you decide to take on . . . pick the battles worth fighting, the ones that mean a lot to you . . . and I believe this one meant a lot . . .

. . . on that Monday morning Kieran lost this one . . . they say he died of multiple organ failure; in truth . . . his heart just stopped . . .

I don't mean to portray Kieran as a hero . . . because he was not . . .
he lived hard, battled hard, died hard . . . so please . . . please . . . go
home . . . talk to the people you love, the people who love you . . .
your friends . . . even the people you meet in the street . . . tell them
you care . . . if for no other reason than because Kieran would have
really liked that . . .

Walk gently through the world;

Do what you know to be right,

Remember Kieran when you have a drink, or drive a car, or get
frustrated with your lover,

Or just can't bring yourself to make that decision . . .

Kieran has not gone away from us . . . he's just gone on before us . . .

They say the eyes are a window into your soul . . . so . . . as you leave
this place to get on with your lives . . . look into my eyes or the eyes
of his mother, his brothers, his sisters . . . all of Kieran's extended
family; the friends whose lives he touched in some chaotic way;
the person beside you right now . . . remember him in your own
special way . . . remember him as he would have wanted you to; but
also remember your own families, and friends and the people you
love . . .

Do you want them to suffer/feel the way you/we are suffering/
feeling now?

. . . mates shouldn't have to bury mates;

. . . lovers shouldn't have to bury the ones they love and . . .

. . . parents shouldn't have to bury their children . . .

Whatever you take away from this service . . . and listening to a grumpy old man rant and rave . . . your life is precious . . . if not to you then to someone who loves you . . . you may be strong, young and fit but you're also very fragile . . . don't stop taking risks . . . just measure them carefully . . .

I wish you peace, love and laughter . . .

May the road rise to meet you as you wander . . .

May the sun shine warmly on your face . . .

And the wind blow gently at your back . . .

And may you rest in the right hand of Christ himself . . .

Thank you for listening, thank you for caring . . .